THE IDEA OF FAITH IN CHRISTIAN LITERATURE

FROM THE DEATH OF SAINT PAUL
TO THE CLOSE OF THE SECOND CENTURY

UNIVERSITÉ DE STRASBOURG

THE IDEA OF FAITH IN CHRISTIAN LITERATURE

FROM THE DEATH OF SAINT PAUL TO THE CLOSE OF THE SECOND CENTURY

THÈSE

présentée à la Faculté de Théologie protestante pour obtenir le grade de Docteur d'Université et soutenue publiquement le 6 juillet 1925

par

WILLIAM HENRY PAINE HATCH

PH. D. (HARVARD)
D. D. (UNION THEOLOGICAL SEMINARY, NEW YORK)
D. THEOL. (STRASBOURG)

PROFESSOR OF THE LITERATURE AND INTERPRETATION OF THE NEW TESTAMENT IN THE EPISCOPAL THEOLOGICAL SCHOOL, CAMBRIDGE, MASSACHUSETTS.

Wipf and Stock Publishers
150 West Broadway • Eugene OR 97401
2001

The Idea of Faith in Christian Literature
From the Death of Saint Paul to the Close of the Second Century
By Hatch, William Henry Paine
ISBN: 1-57910-760-5

Reprinted by *Wipf and Stock Publishers*
150 West Broadway • Eugene OR 97401

Previously published by Strasbourg, 1925.

CONIVGI
FIDELISSIMAE ATQVE CARISSIMAE
ITINERVM COMITI
LABORVM FAVTRICI

PREFACE.

In a former treatise the present writer has discussed the Pauline idea of faith, tracing it back through the teaching of Jesus and Judaism to the earliest Hebrew prophets whose writings have been preserved and to the oldest stratum of the Hexateuch [1].

In the present work the investigation is continued into the post-Pauline period of Christian literature. The books of the New Testament that were written after the death of the Apostle Paul are first considered; then the Apostolic Fathers and the Apologists of the second century are taken up in turn; and finally the study is concluded with Irenaeus's great work against heresies. This is a convenient and logical stopping place; for by the time of Irenaeus's death, which occurred about the year 200, the foundation stones of Christian theology had been laid.

An attempt is made to determine the meaning of the idea of faith in each of the writers who fall within the above-mentioned period, and to trace the development of the idea from Paul to Irenaeus. The various writers are considered, so far as possible, in chronological order. In regard to the authorship and date of the different works, it will suffice

---

[1] See *The Pauline Idea of Faith*, Harvard University Press Cambridge, Mass., 1917.

to say that the conclusions generally accepted among critical scholars are presupposed. This is not the place for a discussion of such matters. On the other hand questions of text and exegesis have received careful attention wherever any doubt or ambiguity exists.

The Epistle to the Ephesians has been considered in the writer's work on the Pauline idea of faith, and for this reason it is not taken into account in the present volume. Nevertheless, the question of its authorship, whether it was written by Paul or by some unknown disciple of the Apostle, is left open.

The Second Epistle of John throws no light on the idea of faith, which is not mentioned or referred to in it. In this respect it is unique among the books of the New Testament.

There are also certain Christian writers who fall within the period under discussion, but whose works, so far as they are extant, contribute nothing to the subject of our investigation. In some cases none of the words which we are studying are found in these writings, and in others the words are used without any religious or theological significance. These writers of course require no discussion, but for the sake of completeness they are mentioned in the table given on pages 1 to 3.

It has seemed best to discuss the fragments of the Kerygma and Apocalypse of Peter, the Epistle to Diognetus, and the recently published Epistola Apostolorum in an appendix.

The following editions of versions of the New Testament have been used: Wordsworth and White's *Nouum Testamentum Latine*, ed. minor, Oxford, 1911; *The New Testament in Syriac* published by the British and Foreign Bible Society, London, 1905-1920; and Horner's editions of the Coptic version in the Bohairic and Sahidic dialects, Oxford (Bohairic 1898-1905; Sahidic 1911-1924).

The Fathers of later times are cited according to the texts published in *Die griechischen christlichen Schriftsteller* and the *Corpus Scriptorum Ecclesiasticorum Latinorum.* If any other edition is employed, this fact is indicated.

In regard to Irenæus a word of explanation is necessary. For the *Adversus Hæreses* the edition of Stieren (Leipzig, 1853) has been used, and for the Greek and Syriac fragments and the Hippolytan additions to the Greek text the edition of Harvey (Cambridge, 1857) has been employed. For the Armenian fragments the writer has relied upon the Latin translation in Pitra-Martin, *Analecta Sacra,* IV., pp. 302 ff., and for the *Apostolic Preaching* upon the German version of Ter-Mekerttschian and Ter-Minassiantz in *Texte und Untersuchungen,* XXXI., 1. He has also frequently consulted the English translation of the latter work by Dr. J. Armitage Robinson (London, 1920).

William Henry Paine Hatch.

The Episcopal Theological School,
Cambridge, Massachusetts,

January 6, 1925.

CONTENTS.

CHAPTER I.

Introduction.

CHAPTER II.

CHAPTER III.

CHAPTER IV.

CHAPTER V.

The Apostolic Fathers.

CHAPTER VI.

The Greek Apologists.

Appendix.

CHAPTER VII.

CHAPTER VIII.

CHAPTER I.

INTRODUCTION.

I. *Table showing the use of words relating to faith in the various writers of the period discussed.*

The study of words is preliminary and subsidiary to the study of ideas, for we can apprehend ideas only by understanding the meaning and use of the words by which they are expressed. We must, therefore, in our inquiry concerning faith examine the use of each of the following words: πίστις, πιστεύειν, πιστός, ἀπιστία, ἀπιστεῖν, ἄπιστος. The table below will show how often each of these six words occurs in the various works which fall within the period under consideration[1]:

(The asterisk indicates that the words are used without any religious or theological significance).

	πίστις	πιστεύειν	πιστός	ἀπιστία	ἀπιστεῖν	ἄπιστος
Hebrews.	32	2	5	2	—	—
1 Peter.	5	3	3	—	1	—
Acts	15	37	4	—	1	1
The Fourth Gospel	—	98	1	—	—	1
1 John	1	9	1	—	—	—

[1] Occurences of the words in spurious passages and erroneous *variae lectiones* are not included in this table. In 1 Clem. 35,5 it is difficult to determine whether διὰ πίστεως (AS) or πιστῶς (HL) is the true reading.

	πίστις	πιστεύειν	πιστός	ἀπιστία	ἀπιστεῖν	ἄπιστος	fides	credere	incredibilis	haimen	shar
2 John	—	—	—	—	—	—					
* 3 John	—	—	1	—	—	—					
Revelation	4	—	8	—	—	1					
1 Timothy	19	3	11	1	—	1					
2 Timothy	8	1	3	—	1	—					
Titus	6	2	3	—	—	1					
James	16	3	—	—	—	—					
Jude	2	1	—	—	—	—					
2 Peter	2	—	—	—	—	—					
1 Clement	19 20[2]	7	9	—	—	—					
Ignatius	27	18	5	2	1	4					
Polycarp	6	5	—	—	—	—	2	3			
Didaché	3	—	—	—	—	—					
Barnabas	9	9	2	—	—	—					
Hermas	39	52	13	1	—	—	—	4	1		
* Papias [3]	1	—	—	—	—	—					
2 Clement	1	6	3	1	—	1					
Mart. Polyc.	—	—	2	—	—	1					
Quadratus	—	—	—	—	—	—					
Aristides	—	—	—	—	—	—					
Apol. Syr.	—	—	—	—	—	—	—	—	—	4	1
Frag. Arm.	—	—	—	—	—	—	1				

[2] Cf. p. 72, n. 1.

[3] The substantive πίστις occurs once in the fragments of Papias (Eus. *H. E.* III. 39,3). He speaks of the commandments which were « given by the Lord to faith and come from (παραγινομένας A Λ Schwartz) the truth itself », contrasting them with the alien commandments of others. He means simply the commandments given by Jesus to his disciples to be believed or accepted by them as true. Lightfoot (*The Apostolic Fathers*, p. 528) translates τῇ πίστει by « the Faith », as if the words signified *fides quae creditur*.

(The asterisk indicates that the words are used without any religious or theological significance.)

	πίστις	πιστεύειν	πιστός	ἀπιστία	ἀπιστεῖν	ἄπιστος	fides	fiducia	credere	fidelis	credibilis	infidelitas	incredulitas	infidelis	incredulus	incredibilis	haimen	mhaiman	Glaube	glauben	gläubig	Unglaube	unglaublich	pistis	pisteye	pistos	apistos	atnahte
Aristo of Pella	—	—	—	—	—	—																						
Justin *Apol. I*	5	27	2	1	6	3																						
Justin *Apol II*	—	1	—	—	—	—																						
Justin *Dial.*	23	78	16	1	2	6																						
Tatian	1	12	—	1	—	—																						
Melito	2	1	—	—	—	—																						
Apollinaris	—	—	—	—	—	—																						
Athenagoras *Leg.*	2	17	—	—	—	—																						
" *De Res.*	5	3	2	4	7	2																						
Theophilus	4	23	—	1	9	2																						
*Ev. sec. Hebræos	—	1	—	—	—	—																						
*Ev. Petri	—	1	—	—	—	—																						
Kerygma Petri	1	4	1	—	—	—																						
Apoc. *Petri	—	1	1	—	—	—																						
Ep. ad Diognetum	2	3	—	—	—	—																						
Ep. Apostolorum																								5	26	1	1	2
*Hermias	—	1	1	—	—	—																						
Ep. Ecclesiarum Viennensis et Lugdunensis	2	4	1	—	—	—																						
*Hegesippus	—	5	—	—	—	—																						
Irenæus																												
Adv. Hær.	24	12	1	—	—	1	116	4	206	20	3	7	6	9	8	2												
Apost. Preach	—	—	—	—	—	—	—	—	—	—	—	—	—	—	—	—	—	—	32	36[4]	7	2	1					
Frag. Gr.	4	4	2	2	1	2																						
" *Syr.*	—	—	—	—	—	—	—	—	—	—	—	—	—	—	—	—	2	1										
" *Arm.*	—	—	—	—	—	—	3	1	2	1																		

[4] 'Glauben' occurs 35 times in the German translation of Ter-Mekerttschian and Ter-Minassiantz. But in § 24 the phrase 'im Vertrauen', used of Abraham, represents the Armenian verb *hawataceal*, i.e. 'believed' or 'trusted'. It is rendered by 'believed' in the English version of Dr. Armitage Robinson.

II. *Meanings of words relating to faith.*

These words are used in the following senses: Πίστις (*a*) *conviction* or *belief*; (*b*) *trust*; (*c*) *faith*; (*d*) *faithfulness* or *fidelity*. Πιστεύειν (*a*) *to be convinced* or *to believe*; (*b*) *to trust*; (*c*) *to have faith*; (*d*) *to entrust*. Πιστός (*a*) *believing*; (*b*) *faithful, trusty, true*; (*c*) *credible*. Ἀπιστία (*a*) *want of faith, unbelief*; (*b*) *unfaithfulness*. Ἀπιστεῖν (*a*) *to disbelieve*; (*b*) *to be unfaithful*. Ἄπιστος (*a*) *unbelieving*; (*b*) *unfaithful, untrustworthy*; (c) *incredible*[5].

III. *The idea of faith in Hebrew and Jewish religion.*

Trust in Jahveh appears in the story of Abraham's colloquy with God, which is found in the oldest stratum of the Hexateuch, and it recurs again and again in the prophets and psalmists of the Old Testament. It is not to be confused with belief in the existence of Jahveh or with some

[5] In addition to those given above the following cognate words deserve mention. Πιστοῦν, in the active and middle *to prove, to confirm*, and in the passive *to be confirmed, to be assured of, to be steadfast*, occurs once in 2 Timothy (3: 14), twice in the First Epistle of Clement (15,4; 42,3), and six times in Athenagoras (*Leg.* 9.1; 32.2; *De Res.* 13 C; 17 D; 18 A; 23 BC). Πιστῶς, *faithfully*, is found once in the Epistle to Diognetus (7.2); once, according to Codex H and the Latin version, in the First Epistle of Clement (35,5); and in one of the fragments of Irenæus (*Frag.* XII). Πίστωσις, *confirmation*, is used once by Athenagoras (*De Res.* 17 D). There are two occurrences of the verbal adjective πιστευτέον, one in Justin (*Dial.* 20,3) and one in Athenagoras (*Leg.* 23,3).

conviction concerning him. Faith or trust is rather the devout man's attitude towards the living God, whose character is known to be such that he can be trusted to the uttermost. It is the heart of Hebrew piety, and it determines in large measure the nature of Israelitish religion.

Judaism developed out of the earlier religion of Israel. At this time mysticism was rife in the Græco-Roman world; but in spite of their contacts with Hellenism the Jews were faithful to the Mosaic law and their ancestral worship, and their religion did not become imbued with mysticism, which was quite foreign to its spirit. Faith or trust in Jahveh continued to be the basic element in piety, and its character remained essentially unchanged. It was still the religious Jew's trustful attitude towards his God.

IV. *The idea of faith in the teaching of Jesus and Paul.*

Jesus was a devout Palestinian Jew. He was born and bred in a pious home and in a religious atmosphere, and from his youth he seems to have been absorbed in the things that pertain to the spiritual life. He lived in the deep piety of the psalmists, and the lofty idealism of the prophets captured and ruled him. He did not receive a scribal education, and he was quite untouched by Hellenistic modes of thought and feeling.

He thought of God as his loving heavenly Father, in whose fellowship he lived day by day, and with whom he frequently communed in prayer. Moreover, the relation between him and his Father was as simple as it was natural. God was wise and good, and faith or trust was the normal and right attitude of mind and heart towards him. Such was Jesus' own faith, and such was the faith which he sought to instil into his disciples [6].

Jesus became convinced that he was in truth the promised and long-expected Messiah, and he demanded of his followers absolute loyalty to himself and his cause. But he did not on this account desire or ask them to trust in him. God should be the sole object of men's trust [7].

The cures narrated in the Synoptic Gospels form a class by themselves. Faith is the indispensable condition of obtaining relief, and faith in these cases is trust or confidence that Jesus has the power to heal [8]. It is not to be confused with the religious man's trust in God. On the other hand when trust in Jesus' power was lacking, he was able to accomplish nothing [9].

---

[6] Cf. Hatch, *The Pauline Idea of Faith,* pp. 21 ff.

[7] Cf. Mk. 11 : 22. See Hatch, *op. cit.*, p. 24.

[8] Cf. Hatch, *op. cit.*, pp. 25f. In Mark's account of the healing of the epileptic boy the father's faith is the ground of the cure (9 : 14–29). Matthew and Luke omit this part of the story. On the other hand, in the case of the paralytic αὐτῶν (Mk. 2 : 5 = Mt. 9 : 2 = Lk. 5 : 20) probably refers to the sick man as well as to those who were carrying him.

[9] Cf. Mk. 6 : 5f. = Mt. 13 : 58. Mark says that Jesus marveled because of the people's lack of faith. He does not expressly ascribe the Master's inability to perform many mighty works in Nazareth to ἀπιστία on the part of the villagers, but this is clearly implied. Matthew, who is dependoea on Mark here, says nothing about Jesus' marveling, doubtless because he felt that the mention of this purely human feeling would detract somewhat from his Messianic dignity ; but, substituting οὐκ ἐποίησεν for Mark's οὐκ ἐδύνατο ποιῆσαι, he declares that Jesus did not do many mighty works in Nazareth because of the people's ἀπιστία. In Luke's account of Jesus' appearance in Nazareth (4 : 16–30) his preaching in the synagogue is emphasized and nothing is said about his inability to perform cures.

Faith or belief in Christ is twice mentioned in the Gospel according to Matthew. In one case Jesus speaks of « these little ones who believe in me »; but the words « in me » (εἰς ἐμέ) cannot be a true part of the Lord's saying [10]. They are an interpretative addition to the logion made by the First Evangelist, and they represent the teaching of the Church of his time.

The second passage relates to belief in Jesus as the Messiah. At the time of the crucifixion « the high-priests mocking, with the scribes and elders, said, 'He saved others; himself he cannot save. He is king of Israel; let him now come down from the cross, and we will believe on him (ἐπ' αὐτόν)' » i. e. will accept him as the Messiah [11]. There is no difficulty here, and hence no comment is necessary.

In providing a setting for Jesus' saying about faith and the sycamine tree Luke represents the Apostles as requesting the Lord to give them faith [12]. Whether the Evangelist rightly understood the Master's meaning is open to question.

---

[10] Cf. Mt. 18 : 6 = Mk. 9 : 42 = Lk. 17 : 2. For a critical discussion of this passage see Hatch, *op. cit.*, p. 22.

[11] Cf. Mt. 27 : 42 = Mk. 15 :32. In Mark πιστεύσωμεν without any accompaniment (ℵ ABCL vg syr-sin boh) has better support than πιστεύσωμεν αὐτῷ (D it pesh sah), and should be adopted. Likewise in Matthew ἐπ' αὐτόν (ℵBL, etc.) is better attested than αὐτῷ (AD etc.) or ἐπ' αὐτῷ (EFG etc.).

[12] Cf. Lk. 17 : 5. Πρόσθες does not mean 'increase', as if the Apostles desired more faith in addition to what they already had. So the Vulgate and the English versions from Wiclif to the R. V.; cf. also Luther's « Stärke uns den Glauben ». Πρόσθες ἡμῖν should be translated 'add to us', i. e. give to us, the request being for something that they did not possess. So the Sinaitic and Curetonian Syriac, the Peshitta, the Bohairic, and the Sahidic. Four renderings are found in Old Latin codices: *auge* (a ff² i etc.), *adauge* (b f), *adde* (d), and *adice* (e; cf. also Iren. *Adv. Hær.* III. 14, 3).

He probably took the words literally and thought of faith as the power to work wonders.

The words of the risen Jesus addressed to the two disciples on the way to Emmaus show that the Third Evangelist, or the author of the source which he was using, thought of faith in Christ as based upon the predictions of the prophets [13]. This idea appears again in Acts [14].

In the spurious ending of Mark faith and baptism are brought into close relation with each other. « He who believes and is baptized shall be saved, but he who does not believe shall be condemned » [15]. The inner principle and most characteristic feature of the Christian life and the rite of admission into the Christian community stand side by side, and the two together insure salvation; whereas unbelief leads to condemnation. Baptism is not mentioned in the second clause; but since faith was normally followed by baptism, the latter is clearly implied. This is one of the earliest references in Christian literature to the familiar doctrine that outside of the Church there is no salvation. Such reflection on the necessity of baptism betrays the relatively late origin of the passage.

Christians are spoken of as « the believers » in this section, just as they are in the Acts and in the epistles of the New Testament [16]. This usage is also common in the literature of the second century.

---

[13] Cf. Lk. 24 : 25. Ἐπί denotes the basis or ground rather than the object of belief. So Meyer, B. Weiss, Merx.

[14] Cf. Acts 24 : 14 ; 26 : 27.

[15] Cf. [Mk.] 16 : 16.

[16] Cf. [Mk.] 16 : 17. On the use of πιστεύοντες, πιστεύσαντες, and πιστοί in this sense cf. Hatch, *op. cit.*, p. 37, note 2.

Paul's background was entirely different from that of Jesus. He was not only a Jew but a Pharisee, and he is said to have studied theology in Jerusalem under Gamaliel, who was the most distinguished liberal teacher of Judaism at that time. Perhaps even in his youth he had some doubts or misgivings concerning his ancestral religion, and he may have desired to hear the best that could be said on behalf of it. On the other hand Paul was born and reared in Tarsus, which was in his day a city of considerable commercial and intellectual importance. Moreover, he travelled extensively in the Græco-Roman world in connection with his missionary work, and by far the greater part of his life was spent in Hellenistic surroundings. It was inevitable that a man of his intellectual power and versatility should be much impressed by what he saw and heard. It was impossible that he should be immune to the subtle influence of Hellenism. Hence it was that two radically different strains met and mingled in the teaching of the Apostle to the Gentiles — the Hebraic and the Hellenistic. The former was his heritage as a Jew, and the latter came to him from the environment in which he lived and worked.

In the Pauline idea of faith there is both a Hebraic and a Hellenistic element. It is at once belief, trust, and loyalty — the fundamental principle of religion and the source of moral excellence. It is of divine origin ; it is the channel through which the Christian derives his distinctive spiritual blessings — peace with God, hope for the future, joy, justification or forgiveness, and salvation. It is the root from which love and the various virtues and graces of the believer's life spring. But faith is also the means by which one is brought into and continues in mystical fellowship with

Christ. It is indeed the mystical state in which the Christian lives [17].

Paul's idea of faith was developed out of trust in Jahveh; but the Apostle to the Gentiles, being himself a mystic and having resided for many years in the Hellenistic world, imparted to the concept of faith a mystical character which it did not have on Palestinian soil. This transformation of simple trust into mystical faith was due not only to Paul's Hellenistic environment, but also to his temperament and religious experience.

---

[17] Cf. Hatch. *op. cit.*, pp. 82f.

Chapter II.

I. *The Epistle to the Hebrews.*

The author of the Epistle to the Hebrews uses all the words which we are investigating except ἀπιστεῖν and ἄπιστος. The substantive πίστις, however, on account of its frequent repetition in chapter XI, greatly predominates over the others.

Faith is an important concept in the work, but it is by no means the writer's main theme. Its rôle is secondary. Indeed, the theological argument concerning the high-priesthood of Christ and the finality and absoluteness of Christianity is complete without it. In Paul, on the other hand, faith is the basis of both religion and ethics, and the idea is fundamental and implicit in all his thinking.

What, then, does the author of Hebrews mean by faith? We must first study his definition, which is carefully drawn up and put before his long list of examples of faith taken from Old Testament history. However, his definition is not meant to be exhaustive. His purpose is practical, and he merely tells his readers in what sense the term πίστις is used. Faith, he says, is « the assurance (ὑπόστασις) of things hoped for, the conviction (ἔλεγχος) of things not seen »[1]. It is fun-

[1] Cf. Heb. 11 : 1. Ὑπόστασις has several meanings and is variously interpreted in this passage. The Vulgate rendering *substantia,* though lexically possible, is not well suited to the context;

damentally trust, and its nature is shown by the effect it has in the lives of those who possess it.

Πίστις in 11 : 1 is contrasted with ὑποστολή in 10 : 39, which is a cowardly shrinking back in the face of difficulty or danger [2]. Faith, on the other hand, is an active principle. It looks to the future, to the things that are not seen but hoped for, and it assures him who possesses it concerning them. Though still future, they become as real as if they were actually perceived by the senses.

Faith of this sort drives men forward and enables them to do heroic deeds, as the long array of Old Testament examples given in chapter XI proves [3]. If any of the heroes or

---

for πίστις is not the essence or real nature of things hoped for, but rather an attitude of mind towards them. Ὑπόστασις here means 'assurance', or 'confidence', as in 2 Cor. 9 : 4 ; 11 : 17 ; Heb. 3 : 14. Luther renders it by « eine gewisse Zuversicht », Tyndale and Cranmer by « a sure confidence ». In like manner ἔλεγχος, which is in apposition with ὑπόστασις, denotes the inner result of proving, not the proof itself (*argumentum*, Vulg.). It is 'conviction' with reference to things not seen. Tyndale and Cranmer translate it by « a certayntie ». Cf. B. Weiss in Meyer's *Kommentar über das N. T.* [6], XIII., p. 281 ; Riggenbach in Zahn's *Kommentar zum N. T.*, XIV., pp. 339ff. ; Windisch in Lietzmann's *Handbuch zum N. T.*, IV. 3, pp. 90f. ; Moffatt, *The Epistle to the Hebrews* in *I. C. C.*, p. 159.

[2] The same contrast is found in Hab. 2 : 4 (LXX), which, like Paul, the author of Hebrews quotes in support of his idea of faith in 10 : 38. ℵ A vg etc. add μου after δίκαιος, whereas the pronoun is omitted by DEKLP pesh boh etc. Cf. also Rom. 1 : 17. The same variation is found in the manuscripts of the LXX, but the weight of authority favours the omission of μου. The variant does not occur in Gal. 3 : 11. For a discussion of Hab. 2 : 4 see Hatch, *The Pauline Idea of Faith*, pp. 5 f.

[3] Cf. Heb. 11 : 4ff. The dative πίστει, denoting the means whereby the end is achieved, occurs 18 times in chapter XI. Διὰ

heroines mentioned by the author had lacked faith and shrunk back through fear, nothing would have been accomplished. In other words, faith is the indispensable condition of accomplishment. It is true that they all died without receiving the fulfillment of the promises ; but nevertheless by virtue of their faith they saw them and greeted them from afar, as one might behold and welcome with joy the goal of his hopes [4].

Noah is said to have become « heir of the righteousness which is according to faith » [5]. This is not at all what Paul means by the « righteousness of faith » [6]. Noah is called a righteous man in the Old Testament [7], and his righteousness consists in the fact that he believed God when he was warned of the calamity that was coming upon the earth, and did as Jahveh commanded him to do. He was righteous because of his faith. Noah's faith was different from that of Abraham, which is used by Paul and the author of James to illustrate and confirm their views of faith ; for in Gen. 15 : 6 the idea is not merely that Abraham believed the Lord when the promise of an heir was made to him, but rather that the patriarch trusted in Jahveh [8]. According to the Epistle to the Hebrews Noah was assured concerning the impending destruction by virtue of his faith, and hence the righteousness ascribed to him in the Old Testament was according to faith (κατὰ πίστιν).

πίστεως in v. 33, which is to be understood with all the finite verbs as far as περιῆλθον in v. 37, denotes the cause as well as the means.

[4] Cf. ibid. 11 : 13. Cf. also 11 : 39.

[5] Cf, ibid. 11 : 7.

[6] Cf. Hatch, *op. cit.*, pp. 56ff.

[7] Cf. e. g. Gen. 6 : 9.

[8] Cf. Hatch, *op. cit.*, pp. 2f.

The writer desires his readers not to « become sluggish, but imitators of those who through faith and perseverance inherit the promises », i. e. receive the promised blessings [9]. The promises are of course those made by God to his people at various times in the past, and faith and perseverance are the means whereby they are inherited. Faith is not mere belief in Jahveh's promises, or even trust in him. It is rather assurance concerning the fulfillment of his promises, which is based ultimately upon his character. Thus in his use of πίστις here the author anticipates the definition of faith given in 11 : 1.

But faith is not merely the means whereby something is accomplished. It may also denote the ground or reason for some act. Thus because of his faith Enoch, the type of the pious man among the Jews [10], was translated, so that he did not have to experience death [11]. He is said in the LXX to have pleased God [12], and the author of Hebrews emphasizes this fact. Moreover, he goes on to say that without faith it is impossible to please God, for he who draws near to God must believe that he exists, and that he rewards those who seek after him [13]. Here, however, the writer's

---

[9] Heb. 6 : 12. D*E*3 insert τῆς before πίστεως. Πίστις and μακροθυμία are juxtaposed in 2 Tim. 3 : 10. For the meaning of κληρονομούντων τὰς ἐπαγγελίας see Riggenbach in Zahn's *Kommentar zum N. T.*, XIV., pp. 165f.

[10] Cf. *Targ. Bab.* on Gen. 5 : 24 (והלך חנוך ברחלתא דיי). רחלתא דיי = יראת יהוה, which is a regular designation of religion in the Old Testament (hcf. e. g. Is. 11 : 2f. ; Ps. 111 : 10).

[11] Cf. Heb. 11 : 5.

[12] Cf. Gen. 5 : 22,24 (εὐηρέστησεν). The Hebrew text has in both verses יתהלך.

[13] Cf. Heb. 11 : 6. The object of εὐαρεστῆσαι is τῷ θεῷ understood from εὐηρεστηκέναι τῷ θεῷ in the preceding verse.

mind has passed, by a play on the word πίστις, from the idea of faith as assurance concerning unseen and future things to that of belief or conviction. In other words, πίστει in verse 5 is used in the sense of the definition in verse 1, but πίστεως in verse 6 is intellectual.

After mentioning various Old Testament heroes and heroines the writer comes finally to Jesus, who for Christians is not only the leading exemplar of faith, but also the captain and perfecter of faith [14]. In him faith found its full and complete expression. « Therefore », says the author of the Epistle to the Hebrews, «. . . let us run with endurance the race that is set before us, looking unto Jesus, the captain and perfecter of faith, who for the joy that was set before him endured the cross, despising shame, and has sat down at the right hand of the throne of God » [15].

Since the Epistle to the Hebrews has certain manifest

---

[14] Cf. ibid. 12 : 2. Ἀρχηγός, in accordance with its derivation means (1) 'author' 'originator' ; and (2) 'leader', 'captain', 'prince'. The word is used twice in Hebrews. In 2 : 10 Christ is referred to as τὸν ἀρχηγὸν τῆς σωτηρίας αὐτῶν, i. e. the author of the salvation of the « many sons » whom god brought to glory. He who was himself perfected through suffering became the author or originator of their salvation. Cf. τὸν ἀρχηγὸν τῆς ζωῆς in Acts 3 : 15. But in Heb. 12 : 2 ἀρχηγόν, as in Acts 5 : 31, means 'leader' or 'captain' (so Westcott, B. Weiss, Riggenbach, Windisch, Moffatt) ; for Jesus is not the author (*auctorem fidei*, Vulg.) of his followers' faith, but the « supreme pioneer » (Moffatt) of πίστις. If the writer had intended the former of these ideas, he would naturally have written τῆς πίστεως ἡμῶν, which no manuscript reads. Cf. the Peshitta *lhaimānūthan* and the English versions of Tyndale, Cranmer, Geneva, 1611 (A. V.), and 1881 (R. V.). Cf. also τῆς σωτηρίας αὐτῶν in bHe. 2 :10.

[15] Cf. ibid. 12 : 1f.

affinities with Alexandrian modes of thought, it is natura. to ask what relation the idea of faith found in it bears to that of the Alexandrian philosopher Philo. The latter's conception of faith has been summarized by the present writer in the following words: « According to him faith stands at the end rather than at the beginning of the religious life, and is the strongest and most steadfast disposition of the soul — the prize which every devout and thoughtful man strives to gain. It is also said to be the most perfect of virtues. Moreover, God is the object of faith, whose positive content is the conviction that he is the sole cause of all things; and by piety and faith it is possible for a person to be united to God. One seeks to attain this ideal state by suppressing his mental faculties and completely detaching himself from the things of sense, that every part of his nature except the soul may become quiescent, and that God may be everything to him. He is transported out of his ordinary self and brought into union with the Deity by a means which transcends the powers of his intellect. Faith of such a sort is mystical »[16]. On the question of the relation of the idea of faith in the Epistle to the Hebrews to that of Philo Professor E. F. Scott concludes that, though « the affinity between the Philonic conception and that which meets us in the Epistle is unmistakable », nevertheless in certain important respects « the idea of faith in Hebrews is different from that of Philo. We have to do with a conception which has its roots in the Alexandrian teaching, but has been transplanted into Christian soil, and in the process has

[16] Cf. Hatch, *op. cit.*, p. 80. Cf. also Scott, *The Epistle to the Hebrews*, pp. 174ff.

undergone a change ». According to Dr. Scott the « significant differences » are these: (1) « The idea of faith as it appears in Philo is closely connected with a theory of knowledge »; whereas « this philosophical interest has no place in Hebrews, or at any rate is altogether secondary ». (2) « The idea of futurity, of which we have little trace in Philo, is strongly emphasised in the Epistle ». (3) « The Philonic conception is blended in Hebrews with eschatological ideas »[17]. Another very important difference is that in Philo faith is mystical, whereas in the Epistle to the Hebrews it is quite free from any trace of mysticism.

In view of these fundamental differences, which seem to the present writer more significant than any broad resemblances in the matter of faith between Philo and the author of Hebrews. it is certainly sound to conclude with Professor Scott that the latter was not « directly acquainted with the teaching of Philo. » Whatever similarities there are between the two writers in regard to faith are satisfactorily explained by the fact that Alexandrian ways of thinking were widely diffused among educated Jews of the Dispersion. In Philo faith is philosophical and mystical; in Hebrews it is religious and practical.

Faith, however, has other meanings in the Epistle to the Hebrews besides the one which has been discussed above. Πίστις is the word for the hearer's response to what he has heard. He believes the message, accepts it, and acts upon it. Thus, speaking of the Israelites and God's promise that they should enter into his rest, the writer says that « the word which they heard did not profit them » because they did not have faith, i. e. they did not believe Jahveh's pro-

---

[17] Cf. Scott, *op. cit.*, pp. 177ff.

mise [18]. On the other hand, « we who believed enter into the rest » [19].

The opposite of faith is unbelief (ἀπιστία), and it was on account of this that the children of Israel did not enter into the promised rest [20]. They did not take God at his word, and they suffered the consequences of not believing him. The result of unbelief is disobedience (ἀπείθεια), and to the disobedient Israelites Jahveh declared under oath that they should not enter into his rest [21]. The writer exhorts his readers to beware of unbelief, or lack of faith in the divine promises, which manifests itself in a falling away from God [22].

Faith, as has been said above, is fundamentally trust, and the object of trust is God [23]. Such faith, together with

---

[18] Cf. Heb. 4 : 2. In spite of the textual and exegetical difficulties involved in the participle συνκεκερασμένους, the general sense of this verse is clear. Westcott and Hort think some primitive corruption lurks here (cf. *Introduction, appendix*, pp. 129f.). Perhaps συνκεκερασμένος (א min pauc d e vg-codd pesh sah), which according to B. Weiss is « exegetisch allein haltbar », was changed at an early date into συνκεκερασμένους (ABCD*M min plur vg-codd boh etc.) under the influence of the preceding ἐκείνους. Of recent editors only Tischendorf, B. Weiss, and Baljon adopt the singular.

[19] Cf. ibid. 4 : 3. The participle πιστεύσαντες, having the article, is attributive, and hence cannot express a condition (de Wette) ; nor should it be limited to a definite class of the believers (Lünemann), for in this case a partitive genitive would be required. It denotes the believers, i. e. Christians, as such. For the tense cf. Acts 4 : 32 ; Rom. 13 : 11 ; 1 Cor. 3 : 5.

[20] Cf. Heb. 3 : 19.

[21] Cf. ibid. 3 : 18.

[22] Cf. ibid. 3 : 12.

[23] Cf. ibid. 6 : 1. Πίστις ἐπὶ θεὸν is found only here in the N. T. Πίστις is used with εἰς θεόν in 1 Pet. 1 : 21 and with πρὸς τὸν

repentance from dead works, the teaching of baptisms and laying on of hands, of resurrection from the dead and eternal judgment, the author regards as the foundation of the Christian religion [24]. Indeed, repentance and trust in God were among the primary demands made by the missionaries of Christ among Gentiles. The hearers must repent of their sins and turn from their evil ways, and their attitude towards God must be one of absolute trust. In no other soil could the Gospel take root.

Religion for the author of Hebrews consists in worship, and worship means drawing near to God. True worship, which was foreshadowed in the cultus of the old covenant, has been made possible for the Christian by Jesus. He, the « great priest over the house of God », « has dedicated for us a new and living way through the veil [25] ». Therefore the writer exhorts his brethren to « draw near with a true heart in full assurance of faith [26] ». The true or sincere heart and the full assurance that springs from faith in the fundamental facts of salvation are the proper concomitants of true worship.

The author of Hebrews speaks of Christians only once

θεόν in 1 Thess. 1 : 8. The object of faith is not expressed elsewhere in the Epistle to the Hebrews.

[24] Cf. Heb. 6 : 2. It is difficult to decide between διδαχῆς (ℵ ACD etc. f vg pesh boh) and διδαχήν (B d syr-hcl). The former is much better attested and is defended by Westcott, Riggenbach, and Windisch ; whereas the latter is preferred by von Soden, B.Weiss, and Moffatt. The present writer inclines to the genitive.

[25] Cf. ibid. 10 : 20f.

[26] Cf. ibid. 10 : 22. B. Weiss (in Meyer's *Kommentar über das N. T.* [6], XIII., p. 264) says : « Eine volle Ueberzeugungsgewissheit (6 : 11) kann der πίστις nur beiwohnen, wenn sie nicht Vertrauen ist,.... sondern feste, keinem Schwanken und Zweifeln mehr ausgesetzte Ueberzeugung von den objektiven Heilstatsachen, die nach 19 ff. die Voraussetzung des προσέρχεσθαι bildeten ».

as « the believers »[27]. Elsewhere he refers to them as « the saints » (οἱ ἅγιοι)[28], and addresses them as « brethren » (ἀδελφοί)[29], or even as « holy brethren » (ἀδελφοὶ ἅγιοι)[30].

The substantive πίστις is not used objectively in Hebrews, as it is in the Pastoral Epistles and Jude, to denote the substance or content of Christian teaching. This idea is expressed by « confession » (ὁμολογία)[31].

In the final chapter, which is probably not a part of the original tract[32], the writer bids his readers to remember

---

[27] Cf. ibid. 4 : 3 (οἱ πιστεύσαντες). The adjective πιστός in Hebrews always has the passive sense of 'trusty' or 'faithful', and it is used in reference to God (10 : 23 ; 11 : 11), Christ (2 : 17 ; 3 : 2), and Moses (3 : 5).

[28] Cf. ibid. 6 : 10. Cf. also 13 : 24.

[29] Cf. ibid. 3 : 12 ; 10 : 19. Cf. also 13 : 22f.

[30] Cf. ibid. 3 : 1.

[31] Cf. ibid. 3 : 1 ; 4 : 14 ; 10 : 23.

[32] Such epistolary character as the Epistle to the Hebrews has is due chiefly to chapter XIII. This final chapter, however, is so unlike what goes before that one cannot resist the conclusion that it was not written by the author of chapters I-XII. It contains various practical exhortations concerning conduct and orthodoxy which are not unlike those found in the Pauline and Pastoral Epistles. Probably verses 1–9a, 17–19, 20–21, 22–25 originally formed the conclusion of a short letter (v. 22) addressed to the church in Rome. The tone and character of this letter were like those of the Pastoral Epistles, and both the writer and the recipients were friends of Timothy (v. 23). It was written after the release of the latter from prison, though neither the arrest nor the release of Timothy is elsewhere related. Verse 8 is an orthodox formula which is probably not original in this context. It serves here as a text for an exhortation not to be « carried away with divers and strange doctrines ». The blessing in verses 20 and 21 has obvious affinities with 1 Pet. 2 : 25 and John 10 : 1–18. The resurrection of Jesus is referred to in verse 20, whereas in the preceding twelve chapters there is no mention of it, though

the officers of their church, and, « considering the issue of their manner of life », to « imitate their faith »[33]. Faith is here the basic principle and most characteristic feature of the Christian life. By imitating the faith exhibited in the lives of these worthies the readers will gain strength to

---

the writer dwells upon Christ's death. Moreover, the idea denoted by the words διαθήκης αἰωνίου (v. 20) is foreign to the author of chapters I-XII. He knew two covenants, the old and the new, and the former, being inferior, was destined to give place to the latter. An « eternal covenant » is something quite different. Verses 22–25 are a postscript. The use of the phrase οἱ ἡγούμενοι (vv. 7, 17, 24) for the officers of the church suggests the Roman community (cf. οἱ ἡγούμενοι in 1 *Clem.* 1,3 ; and οἱ προηγούμενοι in 1 *Clem.* 21,6 ; Hermas, *Vis.* 2.2, 6 ; 3.9,7). So also does the mention of « our brother Timothy », who was with Paul in Rome and hence must have been well known to the Christians of the capital (cf. Phil. 1 : 1 ; 2 : 19 ; Col. 1 : 1 ; Phm. 1). The writer of the letter was probably a member of the church in Rome. Moreover, his exhortations to remember the officials and to obey them and his salutation to them at the end indicate that he may himself have been one of the officers of the church. He was absent from the city, probably temporarily, when he wrote, and some Italian Christians were with him (v. 24). The fragment of this letter which is preserved in chapter XIII may have become attached to the original tract (chapters I-XII) by accident, as the note to Ephesus found in Rom. 16 : 1–23 was appended to Romans ; or it may have been added deliberately, in order to make the tract into an epistle. Verses 9b–16, which are quite different from their context and interrupt the sequence of thought, look like some reader's glosses on the text of the original tract. They were probably relegated to the margin at the end of the Epistle in some copy containing chapter XIII, and were later incorporated into the text. For example, 13 : 10–13 may have been a gloss on 9 : 6f. and 13 : 14 may have been written originally as a note on 11 : 16.

[33] Ibid. 13 : 7.

persevere unto the end amid the difficulties and trials which encompass them [34].

For the author of the Epistle to the Hebrews faith is not merely intellectual, for it is more than conviction or belief. It is, as in Paul, fundamentally trust, and it is personal and religious; but there is no trace of Hellenistic mysticism in it. In this respect the writer is true to the primitive Christian tradition, which, in spite of his obvious Alexandrianism, is one of the basic elements in his teaching.

II. *The First Epistle of Peter.*

Of the words which we are studying, only πίστις, πιστεύειν, πιστός, and ἀπιστεῖν are found in First Peter; and the last-mentioned occurs only once.

First Peter is commonly regarded as the epistle of hope *par excellence* because of the prominence of this idea in it. The recognition of this fact, however, has obscured to some extent the significance of faith in the Epistle [35]; for, as one would expect in the work of a Paulinist, the latter idea is of primary importance. It is not defined, as in the Epistle to the Hebrews, but a knowledge of its content on the part of the readers is assumed. It is indeed a common

---

[34] In Heb. 9:28 AP 31 etc. add διὰ πίστεως after εἰς σωτηρίαν. This reading, which is adopted by Lachmann in his smaller edition of 1831, is no part of the text of the Epistle.

[35] Πίστις and ἐλπίς, and the corresponding verbs, occur as follows in First Peter: πίστις 5 times; ἐλπίς 3 times; πιστεύειν 3 times; ἐλπίζειν twice. The adjective πιστός is found 3 times. It is easy to exaggerate the importance of statistics of this sort, but nevertheless these figures are significant and instructive.

and fundamental element in the Christianity both of the writer and of the recipients of the letter. The substantive πίστις and the verb πιστεύειν are always used in a distinctively Christian sense by the author of First Peter.

No explanation of the origin or beginning of faith is given. The writer does not say whether it springs up spontaneously in the hearer's mind as he listens to the missionaries' preaching; or whether, as in Paul, it is a divine gift. But it must be remembered that he is using a familiar Christian idea with a purely practical end in view. He is not writing a theological treatise, and hence there is no reason why he should explain the origin of faith. He may have accepted Paul's view, or the question may never have occurred to him.

In First Peter faith is primarily trust, and its object is sometimes Christ [36] and sometimes God [37]. There is nothing

[36] Cf. 1 Pet. 1:8. The prepositional phrase εἰς ὅν should be construed with πιστεύοντες, not with ἀγαλλιᾶσθε (ℵ AC² KLP etc.), or ἀγαλλιᾶτε (BC* Or). A lively faith in Christ makes it possible for the readers to rejoice even before his coming.

[37] Cf. ibid. 1:21; 2:6 (= Is. 28:16). In 1:21 these *variae lectiones* occur: πιστούς (AB 9 vg) and πιστεύοντας (ℵ CKLP). The Peshitta and the Coptic (Bohairic and Sahidic) versions may represent either Greek reading. Πιστούς (Lachmann, Tischendorf, Tregelles, Westcott and Hort, Baljon) should be adopted in preference to πιστεύοντας (T. R., Griesbach, Tregelles mg., von Soden, Vogels), which is an interpretative correction. No one would have substitued πιστούς for πιστεύοντας. In 2:6 the author of First Peter undoubtedly wrote ἐπ' αὐτῷ after πιστεύων (ℵᶜ AB vg pesh boh sah etc.), as Paul did in Rom. 9:33 and 10:11, because they were acquainted with the passage in this form. In Is. 28:16 ἐπ' αὐτῷ is read by ℵ AQ; whereas B and the Roman edition of the LXX, like the Massoretic Hebrew and the Peshitta, omit the prepositional phrase. The preposition ἐπί with the dative denotes the basis of trust rather than the object of faith.

contradictory in this, for the attitude of mind and heart is the same in both cases [38].

The end of faith is a more important question from the practical point of view than the origin of faith, and the writer holds certain definite views concerning it. In order to understand the rôle of faith, one must bear in mind that the *parousia* is a vital element in the Christianity of First Peter. In this respect the author is like the primitive Christians of Palestine. He believes that « the day of visitation » is near, and that Christ will soon appear again upon the earth. Then faith will be tested and believers will receive their just reward [39]. This, in other words, is salvation, which is conceived in an eschatological way. The Christian life, which is inaugurated and sustained by faith, issues in salvation; and hence faith is indispensable for those who are to be saved. Only those who believe in Christ will participate in the blessings which will be dispensed when he is revealed from heaven.

It has indeed been foretold in Scripture that he whose faith is based on Christ, the elect and precious cornerstone in Zion, « will in no wise be put to shame » [40]; and the writer

---

[38] Cf. John 14 : 1, where faith in God and faith in Christ are mentioned side by side. Cf. also Iren. *Adv. Hær.* iv. 6,7.

[39] Cf. 1 Pet. 1 : 7. Δοχίμιον is a neuter adjective meaning 'proved'; and here, being followed by τῆς πίστεως, it denotes the genuine element in faith. Cf. Deissmann, *Neue Bibelstudien*, pp. 86ff.

[40] Cf. ibid. 2 : 6f. (v. 6 = Is. 28 : 16). The LXX οὐ μὴ καταισχυνθῇ presupposes לא יבוש; whereas the Massoretic text reads לא יחיש, with which the Vulgat *non festinet* agrees. The Peshitta *lā nedhal* gives correctly the geneeral sense of the promise. For the meaning of ἐπί used with πιστεύειν see note 37 above. According to some scholars τιμή in v. 7 means honour' (de Wette, Huther, Thayer, von Soden, Monnier), and a'ccording to others 'precious-

adds, by way of comment, that the honour is theirs who believe. But, on the other hand, for those who do not believe he is « a stone of stumbling and a rock of offense [41] ». They did not accept the Gospel message when it was presented to them, « being disobedient to the word » ; and the author adds that they were divinely appointed unto disobedience [42]. Moreover, believers are now guarded by the power of God through faith [43], lest on account of the assaults of the devil

ness' (Hort, Windisch). Erasmus, on account of ἔντιμον in v. 6, renders thus: « Vobis est pretiosus, qui in illum credidistis ». Cf. also the translations of Luther, Tyndale, Cranmer, and Geneva, and the A. V. and R. V. (text). On the other hand the Vulgate, the Peshitta, the Bohairic, and the Sahidic take τιμή in the sense of 'honour'. Τιμή seems to the present writer to stand in contrast with καταισχυνθῇ in the preceding verse, and to have its usual sense of 'honour'. Ὑμῖν is a dative of possession rather than of reference.

[41] Cf. ibid. 2 : 7f. Ἀπιστοῦσιν (ℵ BC vg boh sah) is better attested than ἀπειθοῦσιν (AKLP pesh). The ideas denoted by ἀπιστία and ἀπείθεια are closely related, and the two substantives as well as the corresponding verbs are sometimes interchanged in the manuscripts of the N. T. See note 42 below. Cf. also Riggenbach in Zahn's *Kommentar zum N. T.* XIV., p. 92, note 42.

[42] Cf. ibid. 2 : 8. Ἀπειθοῦντες (ℵ ACKLP pesh boh) should be adopted rather than ἀπιστοῦντες (B vg sah). Most commentators take τῷ λόγῳ with ἀπειθοῦντες (Peshitta) rather than with προσκόπτουσιν (Vulgate, Bohairic, and Sahidic). Monnier and Bigg, however, construe it with both.

[43] Cf. ibid. 1 : 5. J. Monnier (*La première épître de l'apôtre Pierre*, p. 37) says: « Remarquer le mouvement de la phrase, ἐν-διὰ-εἰς, dont φρουρουμένους est le lien ». Ἐν is instrumental; διά denotes the means; and εἰς indicates the end. It is fanciful, with de Wette (*Kurzgefasstes Handbuch zum N. T.*², III. 1, p. 32) and B. Weiss (*Der petrinische Lehrbegriff*, p. 189), to understand δυνάμει θεοῦ as the Holy Spirit. Grotius observes: « Per fidem obtinuistis Spiritum Sanctum qui vos custodit in Dei gratia. » On the

they should fail to attain the salvation that is « ready to be revealed in the last time »[44]. Their faith not only corresponds to God's power, but it is also the condition which makes the divine power operative. Even now, by virtue of their faith, they « receive the end of their faith, even the salvation of their souls »[45].

Christianity is a way of salvation, and, as we have seen, the latter depends upon faith. Nevertheless, faith alone does not effect or guarantee salvation. From the Day of Pentecost onwards baptism, however it might be interpreted in different quarters and at different times, stood as the symbol of entrance upon the Christian life, just as faith was the inner principle of that life. In First Peter baptism is a true sacrament and insures salvation; it is indeed a saving ordinance[46]. Faith and sacramental baptism

---

Pauline idea that the Spirit is received through faith see Hatch, *op. cit.* p. 42.

[44] Cf. ibid. 1 : 5. « The end of the times » began with the appearance of Christ upon the earth (1 : 20). Cf. also Heb. 1 : 1 ; 9 : 26. The καιρὸς ἔσχατος, which is near at hand (4 : 5,7), is the last moment in this period. Paul regards the age of Christ as the last epoch in human history. See Hatch, *op. cit.*, p. 59, note 2.

[45] Cf. ibid. 1 : 9. The present participle κομιζόμενοι, which means « receiving as your due », is coincident in time with the verb ἀγαλλιᾶσθε (ℵAC² KLP etc.), or ἀγαλλιᾶτε (BC*vid Or). It refers to the present, not to the future (Castalio), and states « an additional concomitant fact » (Hort). Through their faith in Christ (v. 8) Christians are assured even now, before the *parousia*, of salvation, which is the end of their faith. Τέλος is « id quo spectat et tendit fides » (Castalio).

[46] Cf. ibid. 3 : 21. Holtzmann (*Neutestamentliche Theologie*², i., p. 456) points out that baptism appears here « ebenso als eine rettende Gottestat wie als freie Tat des Täuflings gegenüber Gott ». He thinks, however, that the whole passage is open to suspicion.

are entirely different in origin and character ; but nevertheless the two exist side by side as disparate and unadjusted elements in the writer's thought. In Paul faith and baptism seem to « constitute a single act, of which faith is the subjective and baptism the objective side » [47]. The same may be true in the case of First Peter, but the evidence is less clear. Probably the author had not thought out the relation between faith and baptism. Both were present in Christianity as he knew it, and it is altogether likely that he simply accepted them without sensing any incongruity between them.

Faith and hope, which are both directed towards God, are closely connected in First Peter, and at first sight they seem to be coördinate. Faith, however, is the ground of hope, and the latter is the product of the former. Faith therefore is more fundamental, though the emphasis on hope may be more striking. In Paul also hope springs from faith [48] ; but for him the chief work of faith is love [49]. The author of First Peter more than once exhorts his readers to love one another [50], but love is not expressly connected with faith. However, it is love of the brethren that is enjoined, and all fellow-Christians are sharers in a common faith [51].

Faith is the basic principle of the Christian life, and by it believers are actuated and sustained. The trials of

---

[47] Cf. Hatch., *op. cit.*, pp. 42ff.

[48] Cf. ibid., pp. 54f.

[49] Cf. ibid., pp. 52ff.

[50] Cf. 1 Pet. 1 : 22; 2 : 17; 4 : 8; 5 : 14. In 2 : 17 the whole range of the Christian's duty is summed up in the injunction to honour all men, to love the brotherhood, to fear God, and to honour the king (or emperor).

[51] For Paul's conception of faith as a social bond among Christians see Hatch, *op. cit.*, pp. 49 ff.

divers sorts which are soon coming upon the recipients of the letter, will try and purify their faith as gold is refined in fire, and what is genuine in it will redound to their credit at the revelation of Jesus Christ. Since faith is the inner principle of the Christian life and salvation depends upon it, the readers are urged to resist the devil, being steadfast in faith [52]; for only thus can they overcome their adversary, who is seeking with all his power to accomplish their destruction.

The adjective πιστός once has the active sense of « believing » and twice the passive meaning of « faithful ». Christ was manifested on account of the Christians, who through him are believers in God [53]; and God is a faithful Creator [54], because his character is such that he can be trusted even to the uttermost.

In First Peter faith is not merely belief or conviction. It is primarily trust in a person, and it includes self-surrender. In other words it is religious rather than intellectual. Like Paul, the writer regards faith as the basic principle of the Christian religion; but it has less depth and scope than in the Pauline Epistles, and it is not tinged with mysticism.

---

[52] Cf. 1 Pet. 5 : 9. Τῇ πίστει does not mean *fides quae creditur* (Bigg). The readers are not beset with erroneous doctrines, but rather with moral trials; and in these what is needed is not orthodoxy but steadfastness in the basic principle of their religion. Πίστει is a dative of reference. Cf. Winer, *Grammatik des neutestamentlichen Sprachidioms* [7], p. 202.

[53] Cf. 1 Pet. 1 : 21. Πιστός is used with εἰς only here in the New Testament. For the idea that faith in God is mediated through Christ cf. Justin, *Dial.* 83, 4; 116, 3; 133, 6; Iren. *Adv. Hær.*, III. 4,2; IV. 6,3. See also the addition to Acts 18 : 8 found in Codex Bezae.

[54] Cf. 1 Pet. 4 : 19; 5 : 12.

III. *The Acts of the Apostles.*

The author of Acts uses all the words which we are studying except ἀπιστία. The positive words, however, greatly predominate over the negative, ἀπιστεῖν and ἄπιστος each occurring only once.

The substantive πίστις once has the sense of « conviction » or « assurance » in Acts, and that instance occurs in Paul's speech at Athens. The Apostle is represented as declaring on that occasion that God « has appointed a day in which he will judge the earth (τὴν οἰκουμένην) by a man whom he has ordained, having given assurance (πίστιν) to all by raising him from the dead »[55]. In other words, by raising Christ from the dead God has given men a positive guarantee that he will in like manner raise all on the last day for the final judgment. In view of this future event, according to Paul, God now proclaims to men that they should all everywhere repent[56]; for repentance alone can prepare the way for a favourable judgment.

So, too, the verb πιστεύειν means « to believe » or « put credence in » several times in Acts. However, only two instances of this use of the word will be discussed here, for

---

[55] Some scholars understand πίστις here in the sense of 'faith' (de Wette, Meyer, Holtzmann, Wendt; cf. Luther and A. V. marg.) ; and this may be the right interpretation, for the resurrection was regarded as a proof of Jesus' Messiahship. Cf. Acts 2 : 32ff. ; 10 : 40ff. ; 13 : 30ff. However 'assurance' (Calvin, Beza, Hackett, Blass, Knowling, Preuschen, Loisy ; so also A. V. and R. V.) seems to the present writer on the whole better suited to the context. Page renders πίστιν by 'proof'. Cf. Wettstein, *Novum Testamentum,* II., pp. 572f.

[56] Cf. Acts 17 : 30.

the others are all clear, and there can be no doubt about the meaning. The first case is that of the jailor at Philippi. After Paul and Silas had preached to him the word of God and he had been baptized, « he rejoiced with all his house because he had believed God » [57]. The second case is that of Crispus, the ruler of the synagogue at Corinth. He, like many others who heard Paul preach, « believed the Lord with his whole house » [58], and was baptized by the Apostle himself. The message of Paul and the other Christian missionaries was regarded as the word of God or Christ spoken by these human agents, and hence to accept the message as true was really to believe its divine author [59]. This is what the jailor at Philippi and Crispus did according to the author of Acts [60].

The object of faith or trust as distinguished from belief

---

[57] Cf. ibid. 16 : 34. Instead of τῷ θεῷ D 33 etc. have ἐπὶ τὸν θεόν after πεπιστευκώς.

[58] Cf. ibid. 18 : 8. Κύριος may refer either to Christ or to God. D substitutes εἰς τὸν κύριον for τῷ κυρίῳ, and after ἐβαπτίζοντο adds πιστεύοντες τῷ θεῷ διὰ τοῦ ὀνόματος τοῦ κυρίου ἡμῶν Ἰησοῦ Χριστοῦ. The Latin page of Codex Bezae (d) agrees with the Greek, except that τῷ θεῷ is represented by *in domino*. It is worthy of note that in 13 : 12 D adds τῷ θεῷ after ἐπίστευσεν (*in domino* d), and in 16 : 15 reads τῷ θεῷ instead of τῷ κυρίῳ (*domino* d).

[59] Cf. Hatch. *op. cit.*, pp. 33ff.

[60] According to Blass-Debrunner (*Neutestamentliche Grammatik* [5], p. 110) and most of the commentators πιστεύειν with the dative in Acts 16 : 34 and 18 : 8 means 'to believe in' ; but, as Moulton points out (*A Grammar of New Testament Greek* [2], p. 67), accepting the word of God (or of Christ) as true satisfies the context in both cases. In 5 : 14 τῷ κυρίῳ should be construed with προσετίθεντο, as in 11 : 24 (de Wette, Hackett, Meyer, Wendt, Holtzmann) rather than with πιστεύοντες (Thayer, Blass, Preuschen). Justin Martyr uses πιστεύειν with the dative, with εἰς and the accusative, and with ἐπί and the accusative without any appreciable difference in meaning. Cf. below, p. 105, note 5.

is Christ. Thus Felix the procurator « summoned Paul and heard him concerning faith in Christ Jesus » [61]. In most cases, however, no object is expressed, since it is clear from the context that Christ is meant. Thus in the early days, before the stoning of Stephen, « the word of God increased, and the number of the disciples multiplied greatly, and a great multitude of the priests became obedient to faith » [62]. That is, the priests acknowledged Jesus to be the Messiah and became his followers. The death of Stephen, however, put an end to this rapid growth of the Church in Jerusalem.

The author of Acts attaches great importance to faith, as can be seen from the words which he puts into the mouth of Paul concerning the latter's preaching in Asia. The Apostle's message is declared to have consisted of two points, namely repentance towards God and faith in the Lord Jesus [63].

---

[61] Cf. Acts 24 : 24. Here, as well as in 20 : 21 and 26 : 18, πίστις is used with εἰς and the accusative. In 3 : 16 an objective genitive (τοῦ ὀνόματος αὐτοῦ) occurs, and in the same verse faith is described as being δι' αὐτοῦ. On πίστιν τοῦ σωθῆναι in 14 : 9 see Blass-Debrunner, *op. cit.*, p. 227. The verb πιστεύειν is usually employed without an adjunct; but it may take εἰς and the accusative (10 : 43 ; 14 : 23 ; 19 : 4) or ἐπί and the accusative (9 : 42 ; 11 : 17 ; 16 : 31 [εἰς *pro* ἐπί E] ; 22 : 19 [εἰς *pro* ἐπί min pauc]). In 14 : 23 τῷ κυρίῳ, the antecedent of εἰς ὅν, refers to Christ (Meyer, Wendt, Knowling) rather than to God (de Wette).

[62] Cf. Acts 6 : 7. Cf. ὑπακοὴ πίστεως in Rom. 1 : 5 ; 16 : 26. Cf. also Acts 6 : 5 ; 11 : 24 ; 13 : 8 ; 14 : 22,27 ; 15 : 9 ; 16 : 5. In Acts 6 : 7 Holtzmann (*Hand Commentar zum N. T.*[3], I., 2, p. 52) takes τῇ πίστει in the objective sense, i. e. *fides quae creditur*. But this use of the word seems to be as foreign to Acts and the Third Gospel as it is to the genuine epistles of Paul. Faith is the basic principle of Christianity, and as such it is subjective.

[63] Cf. ibid. 20 : 21.

Faith stands at the beginning of the Christian life and is the basic principle of Christianity. Hence it is natural to say of those who embrace the new religion simply that they « believe » or « have faith »[64], and to speak of them as « believers ». The object of their faith or trust is Christ, whom they believe to be the Messiah[65]. The verb πιστεύειν is similarly used once of some disciples of John the Baptist whom Paul found in Ephesus[66].

Faith ordinarily comes from hearing the gospel preached[67]; but in the case of the proconsul Sergius Paulus the punishment inflicted upon the sorcerer Elymas is at least a contributory cause[68]. Nevertheless, faith is not regarded wholly as a matter of free choice on the part of man. God's providence is supreme and sovereign, and those believe who have been divinely « appointed unto eternal life »[69].

Baptism is the rite of admission into the Christian community, and it normally follows belief in Jesus' Messiahship and faith in him[70].

---

[64] Cf. ibid. 4 : 4 ; 14 : 1 ; 15 : 5 ; 17 : 12 ; 18 : 8,27 ; etc. For πιστός cf. 16 : 1,15. In 16 : 15 the dative τῷ κυρίῳ (τῷ θεῷ D) is used with the adjective.

[65] For οἱ πιστεύσαντες cf. Acts 2 : 44 (πιστεύσαντες ℵ B min h pesh boh ; πιστεύοντες ACDEP min vg) ; 4 : 32. Οἱ πιστοί is used in 10 : 45.

[66] Cf. ibid. 19 : 2.

[67] Cf. ibid. 4 : 4 ; 13 : 48 ; 14 : 1 ; 15 : 7. In 13 : 48 the Harclean Syriac adds τῷ λόγῳ τοῦ κυρίου (not τοῦ θεοῦ, as Tischendorf states) after ἐπίστευσαν.

[68] Cf. ibid. 13 : 12 (D inserts τῷ θεῷ after ἐπίστευσεν). It lies outside the present writer's purpose to discuss the historicity of this event.

[69] Cf. ibid. 13 : 48.

[70] Cf. ibid. 8 : 13 ; 16 : 31ff. ; 18 : 8.

According to Paul's speech in Antioch of Pisidia, remission of sins is proclaimed through Christ and justification is provided in him [71]. The sole condition required for the latter, as in Romans and Galatians, is faith. Moreover, faith in Christ is believed to have the power to cleanse men's hearts and to sanctify those who possess it [72]; but it is not brought into connection with love by the author of Acts. Love (ἀγάπη) is Paul's leading ethical word, and he regards it as the work of faith *par excellence*.

Faith is twice associated with the Holy Spirit in Acts. Stephen and Barnabas, both outstanding representatives of the new religion, are described as being full of faith and the Holy Spirit [73]. Faith is the fundamental principle of Christianity, and the Holy Spirit is the divine power which manifests itself in believers. Paul holds that Christians receive the Spirit through faith [74]. The author of Acts does not say this, but certainly no one could receive the Holy Spirit without faith. Faith normally precedes baptism, and according to Acts the Spirit is imparted sometimes before and sometimes after the administration of that rite [75].

According to the Synoptic Gospels faith or trust on the part of the sufferer was required whenever Jesus performed a cure. So, too, in Acts, a person afflicted with bodily infirmity

---

[71] Cf. ibid. 13 : 38f. In v. 39 ἐν τούτῳ, which corresponds to ἐν νόμῳ, should be taken with δικαιοῦται, not with πιστεύων (Luther). I, the Sahidic version, and the Bohairic manuscript F add ἐπ' αὐτῷ after πιστεύων.

[72] Cf. ibid. 15 : 9 ; 26 : 18.

[73] Cf. ibid. 6 : 5 ; 11 : 24. In the former passage πίστις is mentioned first and in the latter πνεῦμα ἅγιον..

[74] Cf. Gal. 3 : 14.

[75] Cf. Acts 8 : 14ff ; 10 : 44 ff.

can be healed only if he has faith. For example, when Paul saw that the lame man in Lystra « had faith to be made whole », he was able to effect a cure by bidding the cripple to stand upright upon his feet [76]. After the resurrection the power of Jesus was believed to work through the Apostles.

Peter's explanation of the healing of the lame beggar at the Beautiful Gate of the Temple is involved in serious difficulty. In the Greek text two incompatible ideas are combined in a clumsy fashion. It is said, in the same verse, that « by faith in his (Jesus') name his name has made this man strong, whom ye behold and know ; and faith through (δι') him (Jesus) has given him this soundness in the presence of you all » [77]. Was the lame man healed by the mere invocation of Jesus' name, or was the cure wrought by trust in Christ? In the opinion of the present writer Professor Torrey has solved this question. By translating the Greek back into Aramaic he obtains a text which makes perfect sense. « And by faith in his (Jesus') name he (Jesus) has made strong this one, whom ye behold and know ; and faith which is through (*or* in) him (Jesus) has given him this soundness before you all » [78]. This is another case in which a cure is effected by trust in the power of Christ to heal.

---

[76] Cf. ibid. 14 : 9.

[77] Cf. ibid. 3 : 16. The following *variae lectiones* occur in this verse : τῇ πίστει א B min pauc ; ἐπὶ τῇ πίστει א^c ACDEP etc. ; ἐν τῇ πίστει. 119 d e vg boh. The Peshitta *bhaimānūthā* may represent either τῇ πίστει or ἐν τῇ πίστει. In the first and third readings πίστις is thought of as the instrument, whilst in the second it is the basis or ground of the cure.

[78] Cf. Torrey, *The Composition and Date of Acts*, pp. 14ff. Dr. Torrey reconstructs the Aramic original thus: ובהימנתא די לה יהבת בה די שְׁמֵהּ להדֵן די חזין אנתון וידעין אנתון תקף שמה והימנתא לה חלימותא דא קדם כלכון.

God has graciously provided salvation for mankind in Christ, and consequently it can be obtained in none other save in him. The missionaries preach « the way of salvation », but in order to profit by the message one must have faith. In other words faith in Christ is the means by which salvation is obtained [79]. The Christian life leads normally to this goal, and faith is its basic principle and most characteristic feature.

Trust in God appears once in Acts. When Paul and his shipmates were in imminent danger of shipwreck, his confidence was restored by an angelic vision. He trusted to God that what the angel had told him would prove to be true [80]. Such absolute trust in God is based upon what one believes or knows of the divine character, and it belongs to the very essence of the religious consciousness.

Faith is an attitude of mind and heart, and it is the

« Here there is a curious ambiguity in the middle of the sentence which probably accounts for the difficulty in our Greek. What was originally intended was not תַּקֵּף שְׁמֵהּ ἐστερέωσε τὸ ὄνομα αὐτοῦ, but תַּקֵּף שְׁמֵהּ ὑγιῆ ἐποίησεν (or κατέστησεν) αὐτόν. This latter phrase is idiomatic in all respects, and suits its context perfectly, the subject of the verb being either, Ἰησοῦς or ὁ θεός. (In the Greek, the latter would be preferred. Not so in Semitic, in which the change of subject is easier). Luke's rendering is a very natural one, since he seemed to have before him the same word (שְׁמֵהּ) which he had rendered at the beginning of the sentence...... Notice also that the Syriac version renders in this same way, '*He hath made sound and whole*', apparently cutting loose from the Greek and translating according to the requirement of the context » (p. 16).

[79] Cf. Acts 16 : 31. Cf. also 13 : 48. In the latter passage after ἐπίστευσαν 137, c-scr, and the Harclean Syriac add *the word of the Lord* (*of God c-scr*).

[80] Cf. ibid. 27 : 25.

distinctive characteristic of the followers of Jesus. It is based on the belief that he is the Messiah, but it is much more than mere belief. It is primarily trust, and as such it involves self-surrender and loyalty. However, in Acts faith has no mystical connotation, as it does in the Epistles of Paul; and the word nowhere means *fides quae creditur*, the substance or content of Christian teaching, as it does in the Pastoral Epistles and Jude.

The adjective πιστός usually has the active meaning in Acts, but it is once used in the passive sense [81]. The negative ἄπιστος, which occurs only once, means « incredible » [82]. No comment on the use of either of these words is necessary here.

---

[81] Cf. ibid. 13 : 34 (= Is. 55 : 3 LXX).
[82] Cf. ibid 26 : 8.

Chapter III.

I. *The Fourth Gospel.*

The verb πιστεύειν occurs 98 times in the Fourth Gospel, and the adjectives πιστός and ἄπιστος are each found once; but the substantive πίστις is not used. In view of the frequent occurrence of the verb the absence of the substantive is noteworthy.

Faith is of fundamental importance in the Fourth Evangelist's conception of Christianity, but the idea does not have the depth or scope which it has in the thought of Paul. Moreover, in John faith is primarily belief rather than trust[1]. It is the intellectual rather than the religious element which predominates.

[1] It must not be supposed, however, that πίστις means only 'belief'. On the contrary the idea of trust is sometimes uppermost in the word. For example, in 4:50 the βασιλικός, who is probably the centurion of Matt. 8:5–13 and Luke 7:1–10, trusted in Jesus' word concerning his sick son and went his way. Again, in 11:40 Jesus recalls to Martha his saying that if she would believe or trust she should see the glory of God. In both instances πιστεύειν denotes trust or confidence in Jesus' ability to perform a mighty work, in the first case the healing of the sick youth, and in the second the raising of Lazarus. In like manner faith or trust is required for the working of the cures narrated in the Synoptic Gospels. Cf. Hatch, *The Pauline Idea of Faith*, pp. 25f. Cf. also John 14:1 and note 4 below.

The object of faith is almost always Christ, though in some cases it is God [2]. The object is often not expressed, because it is clear from the context that Christ is meant; but on the other hand it is very frequently specified [3]. Sometimes indeed faith in God and faith in Christ are combined. In one passage the Johannine Christ bids his disciples in the same breath to believe in God and to believe in himself [4]; and in another place he says, « He who believes in me be-

---

[2] Cf. John 12 : 44 ; 14 : 1. In both of these passages πιστεύειν governs a prepositional phrase introduced by εἰς. On the other hand in 5 : 24 πιστεύειν takes the dative (τῷ πέμψαντί με). Here, however, the verb means 'to believe' or 'put credence in', (Westcott, Bauer), not 'to believe in'. To believe God is to accept as true the message which comes from him.

[3] Belief in Christ is expressed by the Fourth Evangelist in two ways: (1) by πιστεύειν εἰς Χριστόν (or its equivalent) and (2) by πιστεύειν εἰς τὸ ὄνομα Χριστοῦ (or its equivalent). The latter occurs only three times (1 : 12 ; 2 : 23 ; 3 : 18), whereas the former is found 28 times. In three passages (3 : 16 ; 4 : 39 ; 11 : 45) the manuscripts offer unimportant *variae lectiones*. To believe in the name of Christ is to believe in him in accordance with his specific character, i. e. as the Messiah, the Son of God (cf. 20 : 31). In 5 : 38, 8 : 31, 10 : 37f., and 14 : 11 (perhaps twice) πιστεύειν is used with a dative of the person and means 'to believe' or 'put credence in' rather than 'to believe in'. Cf. Moulton, *A Grammar of New Testament Greek* [2], I., p. 67f.

[4] Cf. John 14 : 1. To take πιστεύετε as imperative in both cases accords best with the context. So de Wette, Westcott, B. Weiss, Holtzmann, and Bauer, as well as the principal Greek interpreters, the Peshitta, and the Coptic version (Bohairic and Sahidic). On the other hand the Vulgate takes the first πιστεύετε as an indicative, and the Sinaitic Syriac renders the second πιστεύετε as an indicative. Πιστεύειν here connotes trust as well as belief. So Holtzmann and Bauer. Cf. also John 4 : 50 and 11 : 40. De Wette and B. Weiss translate πιστεύετε by '*vertrauet.*'

lieves not in me, but in him who sent me. [5] » Faith in God and faith in Christ are inseparable ; for on the one hand God has borne witness to Christ, and on the other Christ has revealed God. Moreover, the psychological act in both cases is the same. Although trust in God is of course a vital and indispensable element of the religious consciousness, it is faith in Christ that the Evangelist emphasizes, for upon this depend all the privileges and blessings which Christians enjoy. It is indeed at the same time the basis upon which the Christian religion rests and the characteristic feature of the Christian life.

According to the Synoptic Gospels Jesus did not ask his followers to believe in him. He believed that he was the Messiah, and they accepted him as such ; but neither forgiveness of sins nor salvation was made conditional upon belief in Jesus' Messiahship. For him and his disciples faith was trust rather than belief, and the object of trust was God [6].

It has just been said that the intellectual element predominates in the Fourth Evangelist's idea of faith. At the very heart of πίστις is the belief that Jesus is the Messiah, the Son of God [7] ; and this conviction is primary and fundamental in the Christian life. If a man is convinced of Jesus' Messiahship, he will become his disciple, and in return he will enjoy the privileges and blessings which only a disciple can experience. The Fourth Gospel resembles the First in laying stress upon the Messiahship of Jesus. For both of these writers this is the primary condition of discipleship. Furthermore, the Christian must believe not only that God

[5] Cf. ibid. 12 : 44.

[6] Cf. Hatch, *The Pauline Idea of Faith*, pp. 23ff.

[7] Cf. John 6 : 69 ; 11 : 27 ; 20 : 31.

has sent Christ into the world [8] and that he came forth from God [9], but also the Father is in him and he in the Father [10].

The faith, or belief, of the original disciples of Jesus, according to the Fourth Evangelist, was based in the main upon three things: the witness of John the Baptist [11], the testimony of Moses and the prophets [12], and the « signs » which the Lord himself wrought [13]. These three proofs ought to convince one that Jesus is in truth the Messiah whose coming was divinely foretold. Indeed the Evangelist's primary purpose in writing his Gospel is to produce this conviction in the minds of his readers, for he knows that through this belief they will have eternal life in the name of Christ. The latter is of course his ultimate aim and hope, but belief in Jesus' Messiahship is the means thereto. Hence he relates the witness of John at considerable length, refers to the testimony of Moses and the prophets, and records seven of the « signs » which Jesus performed. He does this in order that the readers of the Gospel, like the primitive

[8] Cf. ibid. 17 : 8,21.

[9] Cf. ibid. 16 : 27,30. In 16 : 27 L and 59 omit καὶ πεπιστεύκατε — an incorrect but intelligible reading. Cf. also 8 : 24 and 13 : 19, where the words ἐγώ εἰμι, i. e. the one from above, are used.

[10] Cf. ibid. 10 : 38 ; 14 : 10f.

[11] Cf. ibid. 1 : 7, 19ff.

[12] Cf. ibid. 1 : 45 ; 5 : 46f.

[13] Cf. ibid. 2 : 11,23 ; 11 : 45. Cf. also 4 : 48 ; 6 : 30 ; 12 : 37. In 14 : 11, if μοι (ABQ etc. a b ff² q boh) be omitted (with ℵDLW 33 c e f g vg syr-cur pesh sah Tert), Jesus bids his disciples to believe or have faith on account of his works. However, if μοι be adopted, the verb will mean 'to believe' or 'put credence in'. Cf. 10 : 37f. Probably μοι has been introduced into the text from the preceding πιστεύετέ μοι.

disciples, may be convinced and believe that Jesus is the Messiah, the Son of God [14].

Besides the three major proofs mentioned above other reasons for believing in Christ appear in the Fourth Gospel. Thus the disciples believe that he came forth from God because he knows all things [15], just as the Samaritan woman divined that he must be the Messiah because he had told her about her past life [16]. Belief in Christ is produced sometimes by seeing [17] or hearing [18], and sometimes by the testimony of others [19].

Believing (πιστεύειν) is twice conjoined with knowing (γινώσκειν) in the Fourth Gospel [20]. The object in each case is one of the writer's main theses concerning Christ — that he is the Holy One of God, and that he came out from God and was sent by him. Belief is not thought of as inferior to knowledge; for, as we have seen, it rests upon the surest foundations. « To believe and know », or « to know and believe », denotes full assurance or complete conviction [21].

---

14 Cf. ibid. 20 : 31.

15 Cf. ibid. 16 : 30.

16 Cf. ibid. 4 : 29.

17 Cf. ibid. 1 : 34 (ὁρᾶν); 6 : 40 (θεωρεῖν); 20 : 29 (ὁρᾶν). Cf. also 6 : 36. Βλέπειν is not used in this way.

18 Cf. ibid. 4 : 42 (ἀκούειν).

19 Cf. ibid. 4 : 39 (διὰ τὸν λόγον), 42 (διὰ τὴν σὴν λαλιάν); 17 : 20 (διὰ τοῦ λόγου).

20 Cf. ibid. 6 : 69 (πιστεύειν καὶ γινώσκειν); 17 : 8 (γινώσκειν ... καὶ πιστεύειν). Cf. also 16 : 30. In 10 : 38 the reading γνῶτε καὶ γινώσκητε (BLWX 1 33 etc. boh sah Athan) is rightly adopted by all recent editors. Πιστεύσητε, however, is attested here by ℵAΓΔΛΠ etc. f g vg pesh. On the other hand D a b c e ff² l syr-sin Tert Cyp have nothing corresponding to γινώσκητε or πιστεύσητε.

21 For the combination of believing and knowing cf. 1 John 4 : 16; Ignat. *Smyrn.* 3,1; *Did.* 10,2; 2 Clem. 17,5; Aristides *Apol.*

At a later time faith (πίστις) and knowledge (γνῶσις) were sharply distinguished and separated, and the latter was regarded as superior.

The Fourth Evangelist does not associate faith with love of the brethren or other outstanding Christian virtues [22]. He is chiefly interested in the problem of Christ — his nature and his relation to God on the one side and to his disciples on the other. The Christian life with its various obligations lies outside his main purpose in writing the Gospel.

The author of the Fourth Gospel is a thoroughgoing mystic, and he regards the Christian life as a divine life. Christians abide in Christ, and he abides in them [23]. In the parable illustrating the relation which exists between him and his disciples he is the vine and they are the branches [24]. Their life is not only derived from his life, but it is really his life in them. This mystical relationship with Christ is inaugurated and sustained by belief in him. Hence upon the latter the very essence of the Christian life depends.

Moreover, after Christ had been glorified, those who

Syr. 23, 11. In *Dial.* 69, 1 Justin speaks of his knowledge of and belief in the Scriptures (τὴν ἐν ταῖς γραφαῖς γνῶσιν καὶ πίστιν).

[22] In John 16 : 27 love of Christ (φιλεῖν) is conjoined with belief that he came forth from the Father. L, however, omits καὶ πεπιστεύκατε here.

[23] The Johannine μένειν with ἐν is used 7 times in the Fourth Gospel to denote this mystical relationship. The Pauline οἰκεῖν, ἐνοικεῖν, and κατοικεῖν are not found. Cf. below, p. 48, note 53. Cf. also Hatch, *op. cit.*, p. 41, note 1.

[24] Cf. John 15 : 5. The Johanine figure of the vine and branches corresponds to the Pauline metaphor of the body with its members and the Spirit which animates it in 1 Cor. 12 : 12f. Each illustrates the mystical relation which exists between believers and the divine (Christ or the Holy Spirit).

believed in him received the Spirit [25]. The Fourth Evangelist, however, does not, like Paul [26], speak of faith or belief as the means by which the Spirit is received ; but nevertheless belief in Christ is the condition on which it is imparted. It is given to none but believers.

From the mystical relationship existing between Christ and his disciples, which, as we have seen, is based upon belief in him, certain very important results ensue. Chief among these no doubt is « the right to become children of God », which is Christ's gift to « those who believe in his name » [27]. A believer in him will never « thirst » [28], and « out of his belly shall flow rivers of living water » [29]. In other

---

[25] Cf. ibid. 7 : 39. Editors of the New Testament are divided between πιστεύοντες (ℵDXΓΔ etc.) and πιστεύσαντες (BLTW). Tischendorf, Baljon, von Soden, and Vogels read the former ; whereas Lachmann, Tregelles, and Westcott and Hort adopt the latter. B. Weiss (in Meyer's *Kommentar über das N. T.* [8], II., p. 308) thinks the reading πιστεύοντες is due to πιστεύων in the preceding verse. Apart from 7 : 39 the present participle of πιστεύειν is used in the attributive sense, with the article, 18 times in the Fourth Gospel. It is also found once in the circumstantial sense (20 : 31). Πιστεύσαντες on the other hand occurs only in 20 : 29, where it is conjoined with οἱ μὴ ἰδόντες.

[26] Cf. Gal. 3 : 14.

[27] Cf. John 1 : 12. The Johannine τέκνα θεοῦ (or τοῦ θεοῦ), which is used of believers also in 11 : 52, properly denotes physical descent (cf. 1 : 13 ; 1 John 3 : 9) ; whereas the Pauline υἱοὶ θεοῦ (or τοῦ θεοῦ) emphasizes the legal and ethical aspects of sonship.

[28] Cf. ibid. 6 : 35.

[29] Cf. ibid. 7 : 38. This passage does not seem to be based upon anything found in the Old Testament. Perhaps the writer is quoting from some lost apocryphal work. Cf. Weizsäcker, *Untersuchungen über die evangelische Geschichte*, p. 518. Like בטן in the later books of the Old Testament (cf. e. g. Job 15 : 35 ; Prov. 18 : 20 ; 20 :

words he will have his spiritual needs completely satisfied, and he will be a source of blessing to others. Christ came into the world as light [30]; and if men believe in the light, they will become « sons of the light » [31], and so escape the manifold evils of darkness. Moreover, he who believes in Christ will be able to do the works which the Lord himself did in his lifetime — and greater ones, too [32]. In other words the distinctive features of the Christian life, the things that mark off the followers of Christ from other men and constitute their superiority, spring out of their mystical relationship with Christ ; and this, as we have already seen, is due to faith or belief in him.

It is possible that there is one allusion to justification in the Fourth Gospel [33]. But even if the writer does have justification in mind in this passage, it is viewed not from the point of view of faith on the part of Christians, but rather from that of Christ's activity on their behalf in the presence of the Father. He is their advocate (παράκλητος), pleading before God for their acquittal [34]. To be sure they

---

27,30), κοιλία is here the seat of man's inner life. Cf. also Sir. 19 : 12 and 51 : 21, neither of which is extant in Hebrew.

[30] Cf. ibid. 12 : 46. Cf. also 1 : 4f. ; 8 : 12 ; 9 : 5 ; 12 : 35f.

[31] Cf. ibid. 12 : 36. The phrase υἱοὶ φωτός may be derived ultimately from Jesus' saying preserved only in Lk. 16 :8. The expression is Pauline (1 Thess.5 : 5 ; cf. also τέκνα φωτός in Eph. 5 : 8) ; but it is not found in the LXX.

[32] Cf. ibid. 14 : 12. The Evangelist has in mind the various manifestations of the Spirit which were common in the early Church.

[33] Cf. ibid. 16 : 10. Cf. Hatch in *The Harvard Theological Review,* 1921, pp. 103ff.

[34] Cf. 1 John 2 : 1. In the Fourth Gospel παράκλητος is used of the Holy Spirit, but in 14 : 16 the Spirit is spoken of as ἄλλος παράκλητος in comparison with Christ. The word παράκλητος,

are believers, but nothing is said about their faith as a means of justification or as a ground of acquittal.

Salvation is usually spoken of in the Fourth Gospel as « life » or « eternal life » [35], which is different in kind from the natural life. It is divine in origin and nature, and it is unending or everlasting. However, it is a present possession of believers, a life which they can enjoy here and now. To « have eternal life » is to be saved, and so one can be saved in the present age [36]. Nevertheless, the eschatological point of view is not abandoned ; for the hour is coming when all those who are in the tombs will come forth at the sound of Christ's voice and be rewarded or punished according to their deeds [37].

Faith in Christ is the means by which eternal life is obtained [38]. Whosoever believes in him will not perish or

---

which is merely transliterated in the Latin (Vulgate; some old Latin manuscripts have *advocatus* in 14 : 16, 15 : 26, and 16 : 7), Syriac (the Sinaitic Syriac and the Peshitta), and Coptic (Bohairic and Sahidic) versions in the Gospel, probably means 'advocate' rather than 'comforter' in the Fourth Gospel as well as the First Epistle of John. See Westcott's discussion in *The Gospel according to St. John* (1900), pp. 211 ff ; and also Deissmann, *Licht vom Osten,* [4] pp. 285f. On the other hand Bauer (in Lietzmann's *Handbuch zum N. T.*, II., 2, pp. 137ff.) thinks the untechnical idea of 'helper' suits all the Johannine passages.

[35] The relative frequency of ζωή, ζωὴ αἰώνιος , and σωτηρία in the Fourth Gospel is as follows: ζωή 19 times; ζωὴ αἰώνιος 17 times; σωτηρία once. Σωτήρ occurs once, and σώζειν is used in reference to salvation four times. On the Johannine idea of life cf Holtzmann, *Neutestamentliche Theologie,* [2] II., pp. 578ff.

[36] Cf. John 3 :36 ; 5 : 24 ; 6 : 47. In 3 : 36 D has ἵνα ὁ πιστεύων.... ἔχῃ.

[37] Cf. ibid. 5 : 28f.

[38] Cf. ibid. 3 : 15, 16, 36 ; 6 : 40, 47 ; 20 : 31. According, ot 5 : 24 he who hears Jesus' word and believes or puts credence in

die forever, but will live[39]; and for such a one there is no condemnation[40]. On the other hand he who does not believe in Christ has been condemned already on account of his unbelief[41]; and he who is disobedient to him will not see life, but has abiding upon him the wrath of God[42]. However, the Fourth Evangelist does not lose sight of the ethical factor in salvation; for when the dead come forth from their tombs, the righteous and the wicked fare in exactly opposite ways. Life awaits the former, whereas the latter suffer condemnation.

It is possible to « have eternal life » only in mystical fellowship with Christ[43]; and, as we have seen, this relationship is brought about and maintained only by faith or belief in him. Therefore, according to the Fourth Gospel, faith is the sole means by which one can «have eternal life » or obtain salvation.

In the Fourth Gospel faith is primarily belief that Jesus is the Messiah, the Son of God; but it also includes self-surrender and loyalty to him. Moreover, since it brings

---

God has eternal life; for Christ has « words of eternal life » (6 : 68) and his message is from God (8 : 26,28).

[39] Cf. ibid. 3 : 16; 11 : 25f.

[40] Cf. ibid. 3 : 18.

[41] Cf. ibid. 3 : 18.

[42] Cf. ibid. 3 : 36. On the relation between ἀπείθεια and ἀπιστία cf. pp. 18 and 25, notes 41 and 42.

[43] Cf. ibid. 3 : 15; 20 : 31. In 3 : 15 the following *variae lectiones* are found: ἐν αὐτῷ BT^{b}W c g l am fu; εἰς αὐτόν ℵΓΔ etc. a b e f f; ἐπ' αὐτῷ L Thdrt; ἐπ' αὐτόν A. Most editors adopt ἐν αὐτῷ (Tischendorf, Tregelles, Westcott and Hort, Baljon, and Vogels). Lachmann, however, reads ἐπ' αὐτόν and von Soden εἰς αὐτόν. With ἐν αὐτῷ ἔχῃ ζωὴν αἰώνιον cf. ζωὴν ἔχητε ἐν τῷ ὀνόματι αὐτοῦ in 20 : 31.

the believer into mystical fellowship with Christ, faith itself takes on a mystical character. It is indeed the basic principle of religion. However, the Fourth Evangelist does not think of it as the source of moral excellence. The latter consists in keeping the commandments of Christ, and love of him is the motive for so doing [44].

In spite of the vital importance of faith in the thought of the Fourth Gospel, the author nowhere speaks of Christians as « believers », nor does he refer to others as « unbelievers ». The adjectives πιστός and ἄπιστος are each found once, and both are used in the active sense. After furnishing the doubting Thomas with visible and tactual proof of the reality of his body and the identity of his personality, the risen Jesus says to him: « Become not unbelieving, but believing » [45].

II. *The First Epistle of John.*

Each of the three positive words, πίστις, πιστεύειν, and πιστός is found in First John; but ἀπιστία, ἀπιστεῖν, and ἄπιστος are not used. The substantive πίστις and the adjective πιστός each occur once.

The writer assures his readers that « this is the victory which has overcome the world, even our faith » [46]. The same dualistic *Weltanschauung* underlies the thought of the Fourth Gospel and the First Epistle of John. On one side are God, light, and life, and on the other are the world, darkness, and

[44] Cf. ibid. 14 : 15. Cf. also 1 Clem. 49,1. In 1 John 5 : 3 the love of God is declared to be the keeping of his commandments.

[45] Cf. John 20 : 27.

[46] Cf. 1 John 5 : 4.

death. Christ not only conquered in the conflict between good and evil; but he also made it possible for those who believe in him to triumph over the powers of evil, and faith is the means by which the victory is won. By faith is meant both the belief that Jesus is the Messiah, the Son of God, and that attitude of mind and heart by which one is brought into mystical fellowship with Christ. It is through faith that the believer participates in Christ's conquest, and he is thereby assured of victory. « Who is he who overcomes the world but he who believes that Jesus is the Son of God? [47] » Faith is indeed the basic principle of the Christian life.

God has borne witness concerning his Son [48], and everyone must either accept or reject his testimony. He who believes not has made God a liar [49]; but he who believes in the Son of God has the assurance in himself by virtue of his experience [50]. Moreover, he knows and has believed the love of God, which was manifested in the sending of the Son, because he has experienced it [51]. Such a one has indeed been begotten of God [52]; God abides in him, and he in God[53]. Faith, however, is not thought of as a divine gift. To believe or not to believe rests with the individual, and he must bear the consequences of his choice.

---

[47] Cf. ibid. 5 : 5.

[48] Cf. ibid. 5 : 10.

[49] Cf. ibid. 5 : 10.

[50] Cf. ibid. 5 : 10.

[51] Cf. ibid. 4 : 16. For the combination of knowing and believing cf. above, p. 41, note 21.

[52] Cf. ibid. 5 : 1.

[53] Cf. ibid. 4 : 15. The Johannine μένειν with ἐν is used 12 times in First John to denote this mystical relationship. The Pauline οἰκεῖν, ἐνοικεῖν, and κατοικεῖν are not found. Cf. above p. 42, note 23.

Believers have eternal life (ζωὴ αἰώνιος) here and now [54], because they live in mystical fellowship with Christ through faith. He communicates life to them, and that life can never be destroyed by death. This is salvation. On the other hand unbelief, or the rejection of Christ, leads inevitably to death (θάνατος) and destruction (ἀπώλεια). The way of faith is the way of life, and the way of unbelief is the way of death.

God is love, and his commandment is twofold: first, that we should believe « the name of his Son Jesus Christ », i. e. accept the truth that he is the Messiah, as his name implies; and secondly, that we should love each other [55].

---

[54] Cf. ibid. 5: 13. Τοῖς πιστεύουσιν κτλ following the clause ὅτι ... αἰώνιον (ℵ* B pesh) is probably what the author wrote. The separation of τοῖς πιστεύουσιν κτλ from ὑμῖν is paralleled in John 1: 12. The following *variae lectiones* have resulted from attempts to improve the harshness of the style: (*a*) οἱ πιστεύοντες κτλ (ℵ^c A 5 6 13 29 66** etc. vg boh sah); (*b*) καὶ ἵνα πιστεύητε κτλ (KLP al pler arm). Erasmus, Stephanus, and the Elzevirs, on minuscule authority, printed τοῖς πιστεύουσιν κτλ after ὑμῖν and καὶ ἵνα πιστεύητε κτλ after the clause ὅτι ... αἰώνιον. This is obviously a conflate reading.

[55] Cf. 1 John 3: 23. Πιστεύειν is here used with the dative τῷ ὀνόματι, and it means 'to believe' or 'put credence in' « the name of his son Jesus Christ », i. e. to accept the latter as the Messiah in accordance with the connotation of his name. Cf. Brooke, *The Johannine Epistles in I. C. C.*, pp. 104f. The manuscripts are divided between πιστεύωμεν (ℵAC al^{25} fere) and πιστεύσωμεν (BKL al plur). The aorist, however, is to be preferred, and it should be interpreted as complexive. « The conviction », as Brooke says, « is regarded as one fact, not as a continuous process continuously exercising its influence on men. The aorist emphasizes the single fact, without in any way suggesting the length of time occupied in its manifestation. It can quite naturally sum up the action, or

The author of First John, however, does not, like Paul, think of love as springing from faith. Faith in Christ and mutual love stand side by side as the two supreme requirements of God.

In the First Epistle of John faith has the same meaning which it has in the Fourth Gospel. It is primarily the belief that Jesus is the Messiah, the Son of God; but it is also trust in and loyalty to him as such. Moreover, as in the Epistles of Paul and the Fourth Gospel, faith brings the believer into mystical fellowship with Christ, and it is itself tinged with mysticism. It is not, however, thought of as the source from which love or moral excellence spring.

The adjective πιστός, which occurs only once in the First Epistle of John, does not have the active sense of « believing ». The word is used in reference to God, and it means « faithful » [56].

III. *The Third Epistle of John.*

None of the words which we are investigating occur in Third John except the adjective πιστός, and it is used only once [57]. It means « faithful », and it denotes conduct of such a sort as could be expected of Gaius, who was known personally to the writer [58]. It does not signify specifically

---

actions, of a period or of a lifetime, which it regards as 'one act at once' » (*op. cit.*, p. 104).

[56] Cf. ibid. 1 : 9.

[57] Cf. 3 John 5.

[58] Cf. B. Weiss in Meyer's *Kommentar über das N. T.* [6], XIV., pp. 187f. So also Windisch. Cf. the Vulgate *fideliter facis*.

action harmonizing with, or corresponding to, faith in Christ [59], though it has often been interpreted in this way. Hence the use of πιστός in this passage throws no light on the author's idea of faith [60].

IV. *The Book of Revelation.*

Three of the words which we are studying are found in Revelation: πίστις, πιστός, and ἄπιστος. Πιστός occurs twice as frequently as πίστις and eight times as often as ἄπιστος. The preponderance of the adjective πιστός, meaning 'faithful', is due to the fact that the New Testament apocalypse was written to encourage Christians to be faithful to their profession in a time of persecution.

The substantive πίστις twice signifies faith in Christ [61], and twice it seems to mean 'faithfulness' [62]. Although nothing is said about the origin or nature of faith, the idea is fundamental in the writer's conception of Christianity. It is indeed of primary importance, and hence the risen and exalted Christ puts it down to the credit of the church in

[59] Cf. Thayer, *A Greek-English Lexicon of the N. T.*, *s. v.* πιστός; Brooke, *The Johannine Epistles* in *I. C. C.*, pp. 183f. Similarly also de Wette, Huther, and Holtzmann. Oecumenius explains πιστόν as ἄξιον πιστοῦ ἀνδρός, and Vatablus interprets πιστὸν ποιεῖς as *rem facis tua fide dignam*. On the other hand Westcott translates the phrase by « thou makest sure », and he explains it as meaning that « such an act will not be lost, will not fail of its due issue and reward » (cf. *The Epistles of St. John* [4], pp. 237f.). Cf. also Wettstein, *Novum Testamentum*, II., p. 731.

[60] In spite of this fact it has seemed best to discuss 3 John 5 in this place.

[61] Cf. Rev. 2 : 13; 14 :12. In each case πίστις governs an objective genitive.

[62] Cf. ibid. 2 : 19; 13 : 10.

Pergamum that it has not denied faith in him[63]. These Christians were open to censure for permitting certain teachers of erroneous doctrines to flourish in the Christian community ; but the main point was that the members of the church had not apostatized in the days of trial.

Christ is the divine Son of God, the active principle in creation, the suffering and triumphant Messiah, and the Redeemer of his people[64]; and faith is the individual's reaction to Christ — his attitude of mind and heart towards him who is « Lord of lords and King of kings ». It includes belief, trust, and loyalty. The relation established between the believer and Christ by means of faith is personal, and it should be permanent ; but it is not mystical. In other words one does not enter by virtue of faith into mystical fellowship with Christ, as the believer does according to Paul and the Fourth Evangelist.

The author of the Apocalypse was a Jew; and, like many others in the last quarter of the first century, he regarded Christianity as a divinely given law, which Christians are bound to keep. Their faith in Christ lays upon them the obligation of obedience. Hence « the saints » are defined as those « who keep the commandments of God and the faith of Jesus »[65]. Faith in Jesus and the keeping of God's commandments are here combined as the two characteristic features of the Christian life. The latter is moral excellence conceived in a legalistic way ; but, unlike Paul, the writer does not think of it as springing from faith. Faith in Christ merely obligates

---

[63] Cf. ibid. 2 : 13.

[64] Cf. Charles, *The Revelation of St. John* in *I. C. C.*, I., pp. cx ff.

[65] Cf. Rev. 14 : 12. Cf. also 12 : 17.

the believer to live in accordance with the revealed will of God.

Faith, which also includes loyalty, leads naturally to faithfulness or fidelity. The emphasis put upon faithfulness by the author of Revelation was occasioned by the period of storm and stress through which the churches of Asia Minor were passing. The Empire had declared war on the cult of Christ, and no compromise with the enemy was possible. If a believer wishes to obtain «.the crown of life», he must be faithful unto death [66]. In other words fidelity is the condition of receiving the reward of blessedness and glory.

Moreover, when the Lamb shall vanquish the ten Parthian kings or satraps, his army will consist of those who are « called and chosen and faithful » [67]; for only the faithful deserve to share in the Lord's victory.

Faithfulness is conjoined with endurance or steadfastness (ὑπομονή) — staying-power in adversity or suffering, which was a Jewish as well as a Christian virtue. The importance of steadfastness in the eyes of the author of the Apocalypse is evident from the words which are put into the mouth of Jesus and addressed to the angel of the church in Thyatira: « I know thy works, and thy love and faithfulness and service and steadfastness » [68]. All these become

---

[66] Cf. ibid. 2 : 10. Cf. also 2 :13.

[67] Cf. ibid. 17 : 14. Luther rendered πιστοί here by « gläubige », whereas all the important English versions from Wiclif to the R. V. take it in the passive sense. The latter is not only better suited to the context, but it also accords with the use of the word elsewhere in the Apocalypse.

[68] Cf. ibid. 2 : 19. Some scholars understand πίστιν in the sense of 'faith' (de Wette, Düsterdieck, Holtzmann, Swete, Thayer),

the life of everyone who has faith in Christ. On the other hand the cowardly and unfaithful are grouped with the worst sinners, for whom the lake of fire and brimstone, the second death, is appointed [69].

In the Book of Revelation faith is not only belief in Christ, but it is also trust in and loyalty to him. It has, however, no mystical connotation: and it is not throught of as the source of moral excellence.

The adjective πιστός is used of Christ as « the faithful witness » of the visions which the writer records in his book [70], and also as « the faithful and true witness » speaking to the church in Laodicea [71]. He is trustworthy ; his character guarantees the truth of what he communicates, so that one may rely implicitly upon his words [72]. So, too, the Messiah, sitting on a white horse and accompanied by his heavenly hosts, is « faithful and true» [73].

---

whereas others think it means 'faithfulness', (Bousset, Charles, Beckwith). Luther and the major English translations take the former view; but the context seems to the present writer to favour the passive sense. The author is giving a list of Christian virtues. Cf. Gal. 5 : 22.

[69] Cf. ibid. 21 : 8. The commentators are divided as to the meaning of ἀπίστοις, which is found only here in Revelation. Some interpret it as 'unbelieving' (de Wette, Düsterdieck, Holtzmann) and others as 'unfaithful' (Thayer, Bousset, Swete, Moffatt, Charles, Beckwith). Luther and the great English versions understand the word in the former sense. Πιστός always means 'faithful' in the Apocalypse. The ἄπιστοι, mentioned in 21 : 8 immediately after the δειλοί, are apparently those who are « faithless in trial » (Beckwith), or unfaithful in their devotion to Christ.

[70] Cf. ibid. 1 : 5.

[71] Cf. ibid. 3 : 14.

[72] Cf. ibid. 22 : 6. In 21 : 5 « he who sits upon the throne », i. e. God Himself, speaks « trustworthy and true » words.

[73] Cf. ibid. 19 : 11.

CHAPTER IV.

I. *The Pastoral Epistles.*

Each of the six words which we are studying occurs at least once in the Pastoral Epistles, but the positive words greatly outnumber the negative. Ἀπιστία and ἀπιστεῖν are each found once, and ἄπιστος appears twice. The substantive πίστις, which is commonest in First Timothy, is used more times than all the other words put together; but the verb πιστεύειν is of comparatively infrequent occurrence.

Faith is primarily trust, and it is a concept of fundamental importance in the Pastoral Epistles. In this respect they resemble the genuine letters of Paul.

The object of faith is Christ, though in most cases no object is expressed[1]. Faith, however, is not thought of merely as directed towards Christ. It is rather, as in the

---

[1] Paul uses three expressions to denote faith in Christ, and they are substantially identical in meaning: πίστις Χριστοῦ, πίστις ἐν Χριστῷ, and πίστις εἰς Χριστόν (cf. Hatch, *The Pauline Idea of Faith*, p. 46). Of these the first and third are not found in the Pastoral Epistles; but the phrase ἐν Χριστῷ Ἰησοῦ, preceded by the article, is employed four times in connection with πίστις (1 Tim. 1 : 14; 3 : 13; 2 Tim. 1 : 13; 3 :15). In 1 Tim. 1 : 14 and 2 Tim. 1 : 13 faith is conjoined with love, and the prepositional phrase modifies both πίστις and ἀγάπη.

Epistles of Paul, realized in mystical fellowship with him; but it does not seem to be wrought by the Lord.

Faith or trust in God is of primary importance in the religious life, but the idea happens to be mentioned only twice in the Pastoral Epistles. This fact, however, does not imply that the writer or redactor was ignorant of the significance of trust in God, or that he esteemed it lightly; for in the midst of his sufferings he trusts implicitly in God, who is the ground of his confidence and hope [2].

Nothing is said directly about the origin or beginning of Christian faith, because the writer or redactor of the Pastoral Epistles is more concerned with the working and end of faith than with its inception. He is interested in practical rather than in speculative questions. Being a Paulinist, however, he believes in the Pauline doctrine of election, which appears a few times in the Pastoral Epistles [3]. God has elected certain persons to believe in Christ and to obtain salvation by means of faith in him; but it is necessary that they should be awakened and instructed by Christian teachers [4], in order that the election of God may become

---

[2] Cf. 2 Tim. 1 : 12; Tit. 3 : 8. In the latter passage the participle πεπιστευκότες denotes trust in God (Huther, von Soden, B. Weiss, Dibelius) rather than belief in his word (de Wette, Ellicott, Thayer, Lock). The verb πιστεύειν is used twice in reference to God (2 Tim. 1 : 12; Tit. 3 : 8) and twice in reference to Christ (1 Tim. 1 : 16; 3 : 16), and in the two remaining instances it means 'to entrust' (1 Tim. 1 : 11; Tit. 1 : 3). The substantive πίστις, however, is not employed in reference to God.

[3] Cf. 2 Tim. 2 : 10; Tit. 1 : 1. Cf. also 1 Tim. 1 : 12ff.

[4] Cf. 1 Tim. 2 : 7; 4 : 6; 2 Tim. 3 : 14. In 1 Tim. 2 : 7 the phrase ἐν πίστει καὶ ἀληθείᾳ denotes the sphere as well as the subject of the teaching. For πίστει ℵ reads γνώσι (i. e. γνώσει) and A πνεύματι. These are not unnatural substitutions for πίστει.

effective. Human agents are needed for carrying out the divine purpose.

Since faith is the initial act by virtue of which one becomes a Christian and also the basic principle of the Christian life, whatever blessings and privileges the believer enjoys are dependent ultimately upon faith. However, this is not expressly declared to be so in the Pastoral Epistles. According to Paul Christians receive the Holy Spirit through faith [5] or in baptism [6], and thereby they become « pneumatic ». Indeed the indwelling of the individual by the divine Spirit is the central and fundamental fact in the Apostle's conception of the Christian life. In the Pastoral Epistles, on the other hand, the Spirit occupies a place of minor importance [7], and it is not said to be given or received through faith. Faith and the Holy Spirit are not brought into connection with each other [8].

Christianity demanded of its adherents a very high standard of living, and most of them were morally earnest people. Several characteristic Christian virtues are men-

---

[5] Cf. Gal. 3 : 14.

[6] Cf. 1 Cor. 12 : 13.

[7] The Holy Spirit dwells in Christians (2 Tim. 1 : 14, where ἐν ἡμῖν refers to Christians in general and not to Paul and Timothy in particular), and they are inwardly renewed by it (Tit. 3 : 5. where πνεύματος ἁγίου is best taken with ἀνακαινώσεως only). The Spirit also inspires Christian prophets to predict future events (1 Tim. 4 : 1).

[8] In 1 Tim. 4 : 12 ἐν πνεύματι is inserted between ἐν ἀγάπῃ and ἐν πίστει by KLP etc. and appears here in the editions of Erasmus, Stephanus, and the Elzevirs. The phrase is rightly rejected by Tischendorf, Tregelles, Westcott and Hort, von Soden, Baljon, and Vogels. If it is retained, it must be interpreted not of the divine but of the human spirit.

tioned in connection with faith, — love (ἀγάπη) [9], steadfastness or endurance (ὑπομονή) [10], righteousness (δικαιοσύνη) [11], peace (εἰρήνη) [12], purity (ἁγνεία) [13], piety (εὐσέβεια) [14], longsuffering (μακροθυμία) [15], and gentleness (πραϋπάθεια) [16]. By these qualities believers are distinguished from others. Faith, however, is not ordinarily thought of as the source from which they spring, but is rather co-ordinate with them [17]. Paul on the other hand, who has a much profounder philosophy of the Christian life, regards these and similar virtues as the products of faith or the indwelling of the Holy Spirit [18].

A pure heart and a good or pure conscience are several times conjoined with faith in the Pastoral Epistles. Twice the heart and conscience are co-ordinated with faith [19]; and once it is said that deacons should « hold the mystery of faith in a pure conscience » [20]. The general import of these passages is simply that a Christian's heart should be right and his conscience clear. Evil desires, wicked purposes, and a consciousness of sin are out of keeping with faith in Christ, and a believer should have none of them.

---

[9] Cf. 1 Tim. 1 : 14; 2 : 15; 4 : 12; 6 : 11; 2 Tim. 1 : 13; 2 : 22; 3 : 10; Tit. 2 : 2.

[10] Cf. 1 Tim. 6 : 11; 2 Tim. 3 : 10; Tit. 2 : 2.

[11] Cf. 1 Tim. 6 : 11; 2 Tim. 2 : 22.

[12] Cf. 2 Tim. 2 : 22.

[13] Cf. 1 Tim. 4 : 12.

[14] Cf. ibid. 6 : 11.

[15] Cf. 2 Tim. 3 : 10.

[16] Cf. 1 Tim. 6 : 11.

[17] In 1 Tim. 1 : 5, however, ἀγάπη, which is love of one's neighbour, springs from « a pure heart and a good conscience and unfeigned faith ». This is the only passage in which this idea appears.

[18] Cf. Hatch, *op. cit.*, pp. 51ff.

[19] Cf. 1 Tim. 1 : 5,19.

[20] Cf. ibid. 3 : 9.

In Paul faith is the mystical state in which the believer lives; and he must continue in it, in order not to forego the blessings and privileges of the Christian life [21]. So, too, in the Pastoral Epistles faith is the characteristic state of a believer in Christ [22], and if one would continue in fellowship with the Lord, enjoying the advantages and privileges of a believer, he must remain permanently in faith. In other words to be a Christian is to be in faith. Unbelief, the opposite of faith, is the state in which one is before becoming a Christian [23].

Since faith is the most fundamental and characteristic element in the Christian life, Christians are spoken of as « believing » (πιστοί) [24] or as « the believers » (οἱ πιστοί) [25]. Moreover, as was natural and indeed inevitable under the circumstances, faith constituted a strong bond of sympathy among Christians [26]. It united them socially as well as religiously, and it made each one conscious of certain obligations towards the other members of the group. Most of the virtues which believers were expected to practise are social in character.

In the Pastoral Epistles faith is sometimes used objectively to denote the substance or content of Christian teaching. In certain cases πίστις means « the faith », or *fides quae creditur*. For example, the author of First Timothy declares that « some shall apostatize from the faith in later

[21] Cf. Hatch, *op. cit.*, pp. 45f.

[22] Cf. 1 Tim. 1 : 2; Tit. 3 : 15.

[23] Cf. 1 Tim. 1 : 13.

[24] Cf. ibid. 4 : 10; 5 : 16; 6 : 2; Tit. 1 : 6.

[25] Cf. 1 Tim. 4 : 3,12. The participles πιστεύοντες and πιστεύσαντες are not used in the Pastoral Epistles. In Tit. 3 : 8 πεπιστευκότες denotes faith or trust in God. Cf. above, p. 56, note 2.

[26] Cf. 1 Tim. 5 : 16; 6 : 2; Tit. 1 : 4; 3 : 15.

times »[27]. Again, speaking of Timothy, he says: « If you suggest these things to the brethren, you will be a good servant of Christ Jesus, trained up in the words of the faith and the good teaching which you have followed »[28]. Πίστις means « belief » as well as « faith » or « trust », and it was natural that the word should occasionally be employed in the objective sense.

Paul is described in First Timothy as a teacher of the Gentiles « in faith and truth »[29], and believers are those who have known the truth[30]. Faith is thus associated with truth and knowledge, but it is quite distinct from either of them. It is neither belief nor mere intellectual assent, nor is it the means by which one apprehends truth or acquires knowledge.

Faith is the basic principle of the Christian life in the

---

[27] Cf. 1 Tim. 4: 1.

[28] Cf. ibid. 4: 6. It is sometimes difficult, if not impossible, to determine whether πίστις in a given passage has the objective sense or not, and scholars are often divided in regard to the interpretation of the word. Holtzmann (*Neutestamentliche Theologie* ², II., p. 309) takes πίστις objectively in the following places: 1 Tim. 1: 19; 4: 1; 6: 10, 21; Tit. 1: 4. Dr. Lock, the most recent commentator on the Pastoral Epistles, considers the following the clearest instances of the objective sense: 1 Tim. 4: 1; 4: 6; 5: 8; 6: 10; 2 Tim. 3: 8. These cases he regards as more doubtful: 1 Tim. 1: 2,19; 3: 9; 6: 12,21; 2 Tim. 4: 7; Tit. 1: 4,13. Cf. *The Pastoral Epistles* in *I. C. C.*, pp. 20 f. Πίστις does not have this meaning in the genuine epistles of Paul. Cf. Hatch, *op. cit.*, p. 35, note 1.

[29] Cf. ibid. 2: 7. De Wette takes πίστει in the objective sense. א reads ἐν γνώσι (*sic*) and A ἐν πνεύματι instead of ἐν πίστει, but neither of these variants has sufficient attestation to be regarded as the true reading. Γνῶσις and ἀλήθεια are conjoined in Rom. 2: 20, and πνεῦμα and ἀλήθεια in John 4: 23f.

[30] Cf. ibid. 4: 3.

Pastoral Epistles, as it is in Paul, and it is primarily trust — an attitude of mind and heart towards Christ. For example in one passage Timothy is exhorted to « fight the good fight of faith »[31], and in another the writer says of himself: « I have fought the good fight, I have finished the course, I have kept faith[32] ». The Christian life is thought of as a contest or struggle, and its principle is faith.

Justification and salvation are viewed in the Pastoral Epistles from the divine rather than the human end. « But when the goodness and love towards men of God our Saviour appeared, not from works in righteousness which we did, but according to his mercy did he save us through the washing of regeneration and renewal of the Holy Spirit; ... in order that, having been justified by his grace, we might become heirs according to the hope of eternal life »[33]. Justification, which marks the beginning of the Christian

---

[31] Cf. ibid. 6: 12.

[32] Cf. 2 Tim. 4: 7. Πίστις here is subjective (v. Soden, B. Weiss). It is not to be taken objectively (Holtzmann), nor is it to be understood in the sense of 'faithfulness' (Dibelius). Verses 5-8 may have formed part of a genuine letter of Paul written towards the close of his imprisonment in Rome. Cf. Mc Giffert, *The Apostolic Age*, p. 408. Von Soden (in *Hand-Commentar zum N. T.* [2], III., 1, p. 181) thinks verses 9-22, and perhaps also verses 6-8, were written by Paul in Rome after the Epistle to the Philippians; but he believes that it is impossible to determine with certainty whether verses 6-8 are really from the Apostle's hand or not. For faith as the basic principle of the Christian life cf. also 1 Tim. 3: 9; 5: 8; 2 Tim. 2: 18; 3: 8; Tit. 1: 13; 2: 2. In 1 Tim. 5: 8 Lock takes τὴν πίστιν in the objective sense.

[33] Cf. Tit. 3: 4 ff. The words ζωῆς αἰωνίου are best taken as an objective genitive with ἐλπίδα, as in 1: 1. Von Soden, however, construes them with κληρονόμοι.

life, is mentioned only here in these letters [34]; but the idea of salvation occupies a prominent position, for Christianity was regarded as a soteriological religion in Pauline circles.

God or Christ is the saviour of men [35], but the latter must have faith. « Christ Jesus came into the world to save sinners » [36], and eternal life is the end or goal of faith in him[37]. God's mercy moved him to save men, and this he accomplishes « through the washing of regeneration and renewal of the Holy Spirit » [38]. It is the elect, however, who receive this great boon; and the elect are those who have faith in Christ.

Faith is the means by which the Scriptures make believers wise unto salvation [39]; and it is once spoken of as

---

[34] The verb δικαιοῦν is used of Christ in 1 Tim. 3 : 16, but it does not have the technical meaning 'to justify'. He was justified in the Spirit *as* Christ, i. e. he was proved by his resurrection from the dead to be what he really was and what believers recognized him to be. Cf. Rom. 1 : 4; Phil. 2 : 9ff. The words are probably taken from an early Christian hymn.

[35] Σωτήρ is used six times of God (1 Tim. 1 : 1; 2 : 3; 4 : 10; Tit. 1 : 3; 2 : 10; 3 : 4) and four times of Christ (2 Tim. 1 : 10; Tit. 1 : 4; 2 : 13; 3 : 6) in the Pastoral Epistles.

[36] Cf. 1 Tim. 1 : 15.

[37] Cf. ibid. 1 : 16. Faith is thought of as resting upon Christ. Cf. Is. 28 : 16; Rom. 9 : 33; 10 : 11; 1 Pet. 2 : 6.

[38] Cf. Tit. 3 : 5.

[39] Cf. 2 Tim. 3 : 15. Διὰ πίστεως is to be taken with σοφίσαι, not with σωτηρίαν. The Scriptures have power to make one wise unto salvation, if he has faith in Christ; otherwise they are impotent. In 1 Tim. 2 : 15 the writer is probably thinking of Eve (Ellicott, v. Soden, Wohlenberg, Lock), not of women in general (B. Weiss) or of Christian women in particular (Dibelius). Eve's salvation, it is said, will be achieved through child-bearing. « Das

the sphere in which « God's economy », i. e. his training of men for salvation, operates or is realized [40].

In the Pastoral Epistles, as in the genuine letters of Paul, faith is primarily trust rather than belief. In other words the religious element predominates over the intellectual. It is the basic principle of Christianity as well as the most distinctive feature of the Christian life, but it is not ordinarily thought of as the source of moral excellence.

The substantive πίστις and the adjective πιστός sometimes mean respectively 'faithfulness' and 'faithful' [41]; and the negative verb ἀπιστεῖν, which occurs only once in the Pastoral Epistles, has the passive sense [42]. The adjective

---

Kindergebären Eva's hat zur Geburt des σωτήρ geführt » (v. Soden in *op. cit.*, III., 1, p. 231).

[40] Cf. 1 Tim. 1 : 4. The *lectio difficilior* οἰκονομίαν (ℵ AFGKLP boh sah) should be adopted in perference to the 'Western' οἰκοδομήν (D* Iren d f g m [62] vg Iren int pesh). The words οἰκονομίαν θεοῦ are variously interpreted by different scholars: (a) God's stewardship (de Wette, Huther, v. Soden, Lock); (b) God's plan of salvation (B. Weiss); (c) God's training of men for salvation (Dibelius). Ἐν πίστει denotes the sphere in which God's οἰκονομία functions.

[41] In Tit. 2 : 10 πίστις signifies the faithfulness of slaves to their masters; and in 1 Tim. 5 : 12 it means 'plighted faith', or 'engagement'. This is related to faithfulness as the objective to the subjective. The adjective πιστός is passive in the following places: 1 Tim. 1 : 12; 15; 3 : 1,11; 4 : 9; 2 Tim. 2 : 2,11, 13; Tit. 1 : 9; 3 : 8.

[42] In 2 Tim. 2 : 13 the unfaithfulness of Christians is contrasted with Christ's faithfulness, and ἀπιστοῦμεν should be taken, with most of the commentators, in the passive sense. Elsewhere in the N. T., however, the verb means 'to disbelieve', and Ellicott and Abbott-Smith understand it so in 2 Tim. 2 : 13. The Vulgate, Peshitta, and Bohairic versions translate ἀπιστοῦμεν as an active verb. The Sahidic on the other hand has the Greek word ἄπιστος, which in this connection clearly means 'unfaithful'. Unfaithfulness

ἄπιστος is used not only of unbelievers[43], but also of Christians who are unsound in faith[44].

II. *The Epistle of James.*

The author of James uses πίστις 16 times and πιστεύειν three times, but none of the other words which we are investigating occurs. In two instances the verb πιστεύειν is purely intellectual in content, meaning simply 'to believe' or 'be convinced'[45].

Faith is sometimes directed towards God[46] and sometimes towards Christ[47], but the obejct is usually not expressed.

James says nothing about the beginning or origin of faith, whether it is the result of free choice or a gift received from God. There is no reason, however, for thinking that he regarded it as a divine gift. If indeed faith is a matter of free choice on the part of the individual, the writer does not mention the grounds on which it rests. The fact is that he is interested not in the origin or beginning of faith, but in its working, and especially in its relation to conduct.

---

and lack of faith are closely related. Unfaithfulness on the part of Christians springs from a weakening of faith, and in some cases from a loss of it.

[43] Cf. 1 Tim. 5 : 8.

[44] Cf. Tit. 1 : 15.

[45] Cf. Jas. 2 : 19 *bis*.

[46] Cf. ibid. 2 : 23 (= Gen. 15 : 6). Πιστεύειν takes the dative here, but elsewhere it is used either absolutely or with a ὅτι-clause.

[47] Cf. ibid. 2 : 1. Πίστις governs an objective genitive only here in James (τοῦ κυρίου ἡμῶν Ἰησοῦ Χριστοῦ). Elsewhere the word has no adjunct of any sort.

His interest is that of the homilist or practical religious teacher.

He combats with all his power the absurd and morally dangerous notion that a man can be justified, or experience forgiveness of sins, on the basis of faith alone and without regard to his acts. James maintains that faith should « cooperate » with works and be « perfected » or completed by them [48]. « As the body without the spirit is dead, so also is faith without works dead » [49]. In other words faith, unaccompanied by good deeds, can accomplish nothing and is of no avail. This truth is illustrated and proved by the Old Testament examples of Abraham and Rahab [50]. Abraham trusted in God, and the depth and sincerity of his faith were evinced by his readiness to sacrifice his son Isaac. Hence, according to James, the patriarch was justified by works and not by faith alone. Abraham had, as everyone should have, both faith and works. Moreover, the same conclusion is drawn from the story of Rahab the harlot.

Faith and works properly belong together. Faith is completed and manifested by works, but the latter do not of necessity spring from the former. It is possible for a person to have faith without any of the corresponding good works.

It might be supposed that in James faith is primarily or predominantly intellectual, because the writer in his discussion of faith and works passes easily and naturally from faith to belief in the existence and unity of God [51].

---

[48] Cf. ibid. 2 : 22.

[49] Cf. ibid. 2 : 26.

[50] Cf. ibid. 2 : 21ff.

[51] Cf. ibid. 2 : 19. It seems better to take σὺ πιστεύεις ὅτι κτλ as declarative (Huther, Mayor, B.Weiss, Oesterly, Windisch, Ropes) rather than as interrogative (Lachmann, Tischendorf, Baljon, von Soden, Vogels).

Belief is included in the idea; but the basic element in faith is trust, as is clear from the rôle which it plays in the religious life.

Faith is an attitude of trust towards God, and as such it is the fertile soil in which religion and piety flourish. From this disposition of mind and heart springs all true and effective prayer. « If anyone of you lacks wisdom », says James, « let him ask of God, who gives to all generously and does not upbraid, and it will be given to him; but let him ask in faith, nothing doubting »[52]. The same principle also obtains in the case of intercessory prayer. If a brother is sick, « the prayer of faith will save the sick man, and the Lord will raise him up » from his sickness and restore him to health[53].

Moreover, faith must be strong and permanent. It is tried in adversity, and that characteristically Christian attitude of mind and heart may be weakened or even lost altogether[54]. However, the very act of proving produces steadfastness (ὑπομονή), and steadfastness is one of the primary Christian virtues.

The idea of faith in this epistle has often been discussed and compared with the Pauline conception, and the two

---

[52] Cf. ibid. 1 : 5f.

[53] Cf. ibid. 5 : 15. Prayer is here conjoined with anointing with oil. The two are thought of as forming a single act; but « the prayer that springs from faith » is the religiously valuable part. Since τὸν κάμνοντα can only mean « the sick one », σώσει and ἐγερεῖ naturally denote restoration to health. According to some scholars (de Wette, von Soden, Ropes) ὁ κύριος refers to God, and according to others (Huther, Oesterley, Mayor) to Christ. The writer is probably thinking of God.

[54] Cf. ibid. 1 : 3. The omission of τῆς πίστεως by B [3] 81 ff syr-hcl does not seriously impugn the genuineness of the words.

have sometimes been thought to be in irreconcilable conflict [55]. The truth is, however, that James and Paul are not in conflict at all. Professor J. H. Ropes rightly says: « Paul and James move in this matter in different circles of thought, and the attempt to superimpose one circle on the other in order to determine their agreement or disagreement in detail is futile. They can be compared only in the large. Then it appears that the two writers are at one on the moral question; and that the substance of James's own theology is all contained in Paul's, while he lacks everything that made Paul's view distinctive and original. » [56]

James discusses the question of faith and works at some length. His problem, however, and the solution at which he arrives are quite different from those of Paul. The latter deals with the question of justification; and he maintains that one cannot be justified by means of the works prescribed by the Mosaic law, but that justification is possible only on the basis of faith. At the same time, however, he holds that the law is fulfilled through faith; because the chief work of faith is love, and love is the fulfillment of the law. James on the other hand is confronted with the problem of moral conduct and its relation to religion. By « works » he means good deeds in general, and he maintains that a person can be justified only if he has both faith and works.

James thinks very highly of faith, which he understands in the ordinary Christian sense. Indeed faith in Christ is the distinctive characteristic of the believer in Jesus, that which differentiates him from the rest of mankind, and it is also

---

[55] For references to the literature see Bartmann in *Biblische Studien*, II., pp. 1ff.

[56] Cf. Ropes, *The Epistle of St. James* in *I. C. C.*, p. 36.

the basic principle of the Christian life. It is always subjective, — an attitude of trust towards a person; and it contains no trace whatever of mysticism.

III. *The Epistle of Jude.*

Of the words which we are studying only πίστις and πιστεύειν occur in the Epistle of Jude, the former being employed twice and the latter once.

The author of Jude urges his readers to « contend for the faith which was once for all delivered to the saints »[57]; and towards the end of his letter he exhorts them in these words: « Building up yourselves upon your most holy faith... keep yourselves in the love of God »[58]. In the former case faith is something which is to be defended and maintained in the face of opposition, while in the second instance it is thought of as the foundation upon which the addressees' spiritual life is to be reared. In both cases πίστις is objective, and it denotes the substance or content of Christian teaching, — *fides quae creditur*. It is not, however, a system or body of doctrine[59]. Πίστις means 'belief' as well as 'trust'; and hence the word, passing from the subjective to the objective sense, came easily and naturally to mean that

---

[57] Cf. Jude 3.

[58] Cf. ibid. 20. Cf. also *Polyc.* 3,2; 4,2.

[59] Seeberg (*Der Katechismus der Urchristenheit*, pp. 195 f.) thinks τῇ ... πίστει can refer only to a formula of faith (*Glaubensformel*). « The faith », according to the author of Jude, is a norm or standard of truth; but there is no evidence that he was thinking of a definitive formula of the Christian faith (*regula fidei*).

which is believed. The religious meaning of πίστις does not figure in this development.

Faith or trust in God is of fundamental importance, as the history of Israel clearly shows. For after the Lord had rescued his people out of Egypt, « he destroyed those who did not have faith »[60]. Lack of faith is punished with great severity.

IV. *The Second Epistle of Peter.*

Of the words which we are investigating the author of Second Peter uses only the substantive πίστις, which occurs twice; and in both cases it denotes faith in reference to Christ, though no object is expressed.

Nothing is said about the beginning of faith; but it is clearly conceived as a divine gift, a precious possession

---

[60] Cf. ibid. 5. The following *variae lectiones* are found in this verse: κύριος C* vid (praem. ὁ KL syr-hcl); Ἰησοῦς AB min vg boh sah; ὁ θεός C [2] min pesh. The choice lies between κύριος and Ἰησοῦς, and probability favours the former. So Scholz, Tischendorf, Tregelles, Westcott and Hort, Baljon, von Soden, and Vogels; but Griesbach and Lachmann prefer Ἰησοῦς, and Tregelles and Westcott and Hort print it in the margin. If we assume that κύριος is the right reading, Ἰησοῦς and ὁ θεός are easily explained as divergent interpretations of it. They are probably glosses which in some copies supplanted the original word. By κύριος the author probably means God; but it is possible that Ἰησοῦς rightly represents his meaning, for in the second century many of the things narrated in the O. T. were believed to have been done by Christ before he was born into this world. For a different explanation of the textual problem, see Westcott and Hort, *Introduction, appendix*, p. 106.

which Christians have obtained through the justice of Christ [61]. However, faith does not bring the believer into mystical fellowship with Christ, nor does it seem to have any mystical connotation. Concerning the end or issue of faith the author of the epistle is silent.

Faith is mentioned first among several impoıtant Christian concepts — virtue (ἀρετή), knowledge (γνῶσις), self-control (ἐγκράτεια), steadfastness (ὑπομονή), piety (εὐσέβεια), love of the brethren (φιλαδελφία), and love (ἀγάπη) [62]; but faith is not thought of as the root from which the others spring [63]. It is simply pre-eminent among those virtues or possessions

---

[61] Cf. 2 Pet. 1 : 1. Λαχοῦσιν indicates that faith is a divine gift. Cf. Huther in Meyer's *Kommentar über das N. T.* [4], XII., p. 341; and Mayor, *The Epistle of St. Jude and the Second Epistle of St. Peter*, p. 81. According to von Soden (*Hand-Commentar zum N. T.* [3], III., 2, p. 214) and Knopf (in Meyer's *Kommentar über das N. T.* [7], XII., p. 259) πίστις is objective. But in verse 5 πίστει is clearly subjective, and the present writer sees no reason for interpreting the word objectively in verse 1. The use of the verb λαγχάνειν is not decisive. The phrase τοῦ θεοῦ ἡμῶν καὶ σωτῆρος Ἰησοῦ Χριστοῦ refers to Christ only, not to God and Christ. Cf. Blass-Debrunner, *Grammatik des neutestamentlichen Griechisch* [5], p. 159. Cf. Tit. 2 :13. Κυρίου (א 9 68 pesh sah) is obviously a correction.

[62] Cf. ibid. 1 : 5ff. The series is not logically arranged. The writer has simply brought together eight prominent Christian concepts and set them down one after the other. For similar lists see 2 Cor. 6 : 4ff.; Gal. 5 : 22f.; 1 Tim. 6 : 11; Apoc. 2 : 19; 1 Clem. 62,2; *Barn.* 2, 2f. See also Dittenberger, *Orientis Graeci Inscriptiones Selectæ*, II., pp. 12f., (no. 438).

[63] Von Soden (*op. cit.*, III., 2, p. 216) regards faith as « the root of all the following virtues »; and Mayor (*op. cit.*, p. 90) says that « faith is the foundation of a series of seven virtues ». These conclusions, however, do not seem to be warranted by the author's language.

which are characteristic of the Christian life. Nevertheless, without faith no one can be a Christian.

In Second Peter faith is primarily trust, but it also includes belief in and loyalty to Christ. It is not, however, as it is in the Epistles of Paul, the fundamental principle of Christianity; for in Second Peter the Christian religion is based upon the knowledge (ἐπίγνωσις) of God and Christ [64]. Christianity is indeed the true gnosis, and as such it is superior to every other form of religious teaching.

[64] Cf. 2 Pet. 1 : 2f., 8; 2 : 20. Cf. also Holtzmann, *Neutestamentliche Theologie* [2], II., p. 366.

CHAPTER V.

THE APOSTOLIC FATHERS.

I. *Clement of Rome.*

Clement of Rome has much in common with Paul, and hence it is not at all surprising that the idea of faith should occupy a prominent place in his throught. Πίστις, πιστεύειν, and πιστός are found in First Clement, πίστις being of much more frequent occurence than either of the others. The negative words, as it happens, are not used.

The object of faith, though it is usually unexpressed, is sometimes Christ and sometimes God [1]; and faith itself,

[1] Πίστις twice takes an objective genitive, which in both cases refers to God (3,4; 27,3). However, in 27,3 ἡ πίστις αὐτοῦ may mean 'his faithfulness' (cf. Knopf in Lietzmann's *Handbuch zum N. T., Ergänzungsband,* I., p. 91). The phrase ἡ ἐν Χριστῷ πίστις (cf. Eph. 1 : 15 and Col. 1 : 4) occurs once (22, 1). In 35,5, according to Codex Alexandrinus and the Syriac version (the Coptic is defective at this point), the prepositional phrase διὰ πίστεως is used, being followed immediately by πρὸς τὸν θεόν; but Codex Hierosolymitanus, with which the Latin version agrees, reads πιστῶς. Gebhardt-Harnack, Funk, and Lake adopt the latter. If, however, the former reading be accepted (with Lightfoot), πρὸς τὸν θεόν is most naturally taken with πίστεως. The verb πιστεύειν is construed with the dative (10,6), with ἐπί and the dative (34,4), and with ἐπί and the accusative (12,7).

as in Paul, is primarily trust. Clement, however, does not think of faith as the means by which believers are brought into mystical fellowship with Christ or God [2]. Faith indeed is quite free from any trace of mysticism.

Faith marks the beginning of the Christian life. God is supreme and sovereign, and it is he who elects and calls Christians. Nevertheless, faith is indispensable in every case; for, in its initial stage, it is the individual's response to God's gracious act of electing and calling him to be a Christian. By faith the believer coöperates with God. Faith no doubt arises from hearing the Gospel preached, though this is not expressly stated. Clement, unlike Paul, does not seem to regard faith as a divine gift.

According to Clement a man is justified through faith alone, which, as has been said above, is primarily trust. « We are not justified through ourselves or through our own wisdom or understanding or piety or works which we have wrought in holiness of heart, but through faith, through which the almighty God has justified all men who have been from the beginning »[3]. Nevertheless, shortly before this he exhorts his readers to refrain from certain evil practices, « being justified by works and not by words » [4]. The inconsistency between these two views is ignored. Justification,

---

[2] In 22,1 faith is experienced in fellowship with the 'pneumatic' Christ.

[3] Cf. 1 Clem. 32,4. The « works » referred to here are not ἔργα τοῦ νόμου, but, as in James, good conduct in general. The Mosaic law and its works, apart from the Decalogue, were no longer matters of controversy or even of interest to Christians in the last decade of the first century.

[4] Cf. ibid. 30,3. The opposition of works and words (ἔργα καὶ λόγοι) is found in classical Greek literature. Cf. e. g. Soph. *El.* 357f.; Eur. *Alc.* 339; Thuc. 1. 78,3. Cf. also Mt. 23: 3.

which is mentioned in connection with the divine call to salvation in Christ, comes near the beginning of the Christian life and makes the believer's subsequent moral and spiritual development possible. It is thus of fundamental importance in the writer's view of Christianity.

Clement refers to the faith of Abraham and of Rahab, but he does not use either of these Old Testament figures to illustrate or confirm his view concerning justification. Abraham was rewarded with a son in his old age « on account of his faith and hospitality »[5], and he was blessed « because he wrought righteousness and truth through faith »[6]. It was on account of her faith and hospitality that Rahab was saved from the destruction which befell Jericho[7].

The Christian life is one of moral earnestness, and certain virtues are characteristic of it. Many of these are mentioned, e. g. love (ἀγάπη), peace (εἰρήνη), gentleness (πραΰτης), humility (ταπεινοφροσύνη), hospitality(φιλοξενία), and purity (ἁγνεία). Faith should be accompanied by good conduct[8], and several outstanding Christian virtues are associated with it, — love (ἀγάπη)[9], hope (ἐλπίς)[10], self-control (ἐγκράτεια)[11], sobriety (σωφροσύνη)[12], endurance (ὑπομονή)[13], long-suffering (μακροθυμία)[14], peace

[5] Cf. ibid. 10,7.

[6] Cf. ibid. 31,2.

[7] Cf. ibid. 12,1.

[8] Cf. ibid 31,2 ; 34,4.

[9] Cf ibid. 2,2.

[10] Cf. ibid. 58,2.

[11] Cf ibid. 62,2 ; 64.

[12] Cf. ibid. 62,2 ; 64.

[13] Cf. ibid. 62,2 ; 64.

[14] Cf. ibid. 64.

(εἰρήνη)[15], fear (φόβος)[16], purity (ἁγνεία)[17], and hospitality (φιλοξενία)[18]. The Pauline triad of faith, hope, and love does not occur. Clement, however, does not regard these various Christian virtues as springing from faith. The latter is not, as it is in Paul, the source of moral excellence.

Faith and repentance are mentioned together among the things « which become our religion and are most useful for a virtuous life »[19], but their relation to each other is not explained. So, too, the fathers are spoken of as having called on God « holily in faith and truth »[20]. In other words, faith and truth are the sphere in which those ancient worthies made their requests known to God. Faith is trust, — that attitude of mind and heart which is the primary requisit for all genuine prayer and worship.

Sanctification, which is the ideal of the Christian life on its ethical side, is mentioned by Clement along with the call to salvation in Christ. Christians are called and sanctified « by (ἐν) the will of God through our Lord Jesus Christ »[21]. Sanctification to be sure is not expressly connected with faith. Nevertheless, like everything else that is characteristic of the Christian life, it is indirectly dependent upon faith in Christ.

Salvation has been made possible by the death of Christ upon the cross. His blood was shed « for our salvation »[22], and « through the blood of the Lord there will be redemption

---

[15] Cf. ibid. 64.
[16] Cf ibid. 64.
[17] Cf ibid. 64.
[18] Cf. ibid. 10,7; 12,1.
[19] Cf. ibid. 62,1 f.
[20] Cf. ibid. 60,4. Cf. 1 Tim. 2:7.
[21] Cf. I Clem. *prooem.*
[22] Cf. ibid. 7,4.

for all who believe and hope on God »[23]. Jesus Christ is « the way in which we found our salvation »[24]. It goes without saying that faith is necessary in order to secure the benefits of Christ's death; for if one does not believe in him, one cannot hope to participate in the Lord's saving work for mankind.

Furthermore, one must repent and act in accordance with the commandments of God, if one wishes to be « enrolled and reckoned in the number of those who are saved through Jesus Christ »[25].

Πίστις is once used objectively of the persons of the Trinity. God, Christ, and the Holy Spirit are spoken of as « the faith and the hope of the elect »[26]. Elsewhere, however, the word denotes an attitude of trust towards Christ or God. It is nowhere used in the sense of « the faith », i. e. the substance or content of Christian teaching.

The adjective πιστός means sometimes 'believing' and sometimes 'faithful' ; but in spite of the fundamental importance ascribed to faith, Christians are not called 'the believers' (οἱ πιστοί).

II. *Ignatius.*

The thought of Ignatius is based to a great extent upon that of Paul, whose Epistles he frequently quotes. Both are mystics, and in the matter of temperament they are not altogether dissimilar. Faith is a prominent idea

---

[23] Cf. ibid. 12,7.
[24] Cf. ibid. 36,1.
[25] Cf. ibid. 7,5ff.; 58,2.
[26] Cf. ibid. 58,2.

in the letters of Ignatius, but it lacks the depth which it has in Paul.

Ignatius uses all the words which we are studying. Πίστις and πιστεύειν, however, naturally predominate over the others.

The object of faith is usually unexpressed, but it is almost always understood to be Christ. In a few passages he is expressly mentioned as the object of faith [27]. Πίστις, however, is directed not only towards Christ, but also towards his grace [28], his blood [29], and his death [30]; for these, as well as his person, have religious or theological significance. Not even once is God the object of faith [31].

In the Epistles of Ignatius, as in those of the Apostle Paul, the religious element in faith is uppermost. It is trust ather than mere belief [32], and it involves self-surrender and

---

[27] For πίστις with an objective genitive cf. *Eph.* 20,1; *Mag.* 1,1. In *Rom. init.* G [2], A[2], and K (Sahidic) have πίστιν καὶ ἀγάπην Ἰησοῦ Χριστοῦ; but G[1], L[1], and Symeon Metaphrastes omit πίστιν. Lightfoot adopts the longer reading; but Zahn, Funk, and Lake rightly reject πίστιν and read ἀγάπην Ἰησοῦ Χριστοῦ. For πιστεύειν with the dative of the person cf. *Trall.* 9,2. In *Eph.* 14,1 the phrase εἰς Ἰησοῦν Χριστὸν ἔχειν τὴν πίστιν occurs; and in *Philad.* 8,2 faith is spoken of as being through him (δι' αὐτοῦ).

[28] Cf. *Philad.* 8,1. Cf. also *Polyc.* 7,3.

[29] Cf. *Smyrn.* 6,1.

[30] Cf. *Trall.* 2,1.

[31] In *Eph.* 16,2 θεοῦ in the phrase πίστιν θεοῦ is not an objective genitive. Cf. Zahn in Gebhardt, Harnack, and Zahn, *Patrum Apostolicorum Opera*, II., p. 21.

[32] In *Smyrn.* 3,1 Ignatius uses the expression εἰδέναι καὶ πιστεύειν to denote full and complete assurance. The phrase does not occur elsewhere in the epistles. Cf. the Johannine phrase πιστεύειν καὶ γινώσκειν (John 6 : 69).

loyalty. It is the religious man's attitude of mind and heart towards Christ and God. Πίστις in Ignatius is always subjective. It never has the objective sense of *fides quae creditur* [33].

According to Ignatius faith is based upon belief in the death of Christ [34], which, however, is connected with his resurrection from the dead. It is true that the prophets foretold Christ and looked forward with hope to his coming [35], but their predictions are not regarded as the basis of faith in him. Nor are the miracles which he wrought during his ministry narrated or even referred to as a reason for believing in him. Moreover, faith is not, as it is in Paul, a divine gift. It is simply an exercise of the individual's will.

Faith is the basic and most characteristic element in Christianity, and it is often mentioned along with certain Christian virtues. Ignatius is especially fond of the combination of faith and love (ἀγάπη) [36], but he does not think of the latter as being dependent upon the former. « Your

---

[33] In *Eph.* 10,2 Lightfoot and Lake render τῇ πίστει by « the faith ». But, as in Col. 1 : 23, the subjective sense suits the context quite as well as the objective, and it accords with Ignatius's use of πίστις in other passages. In *Smyrn.* 10,2 Christ is spoken of as ἡ τελεία πίστις (G^1 L^1). Lightfoot takes πίστις in the passive sense of 'faithfulness' — a meaning of the word not found elsewhere in the Ignatian Epistles. If the reading is right, it probably means 'faith' (so Bauer). Lake on the other hand adopts ἐλπίς (G^2 B A), which occurs several times in Ignatius as a designation of Christ. Cf. *Eph.* 21,2 ; *Mag.* 11 ; *Trall. init.* ; 2,2 ; *Philad.* 11,2. The idea is Pauline. Cf. Col. 1 : 27.

[34] Cf. *Eph.* 16,2 ; *Mag.* 9,2 ; *Trall.* 2,1.

[35] Cf. *Philad.* 5,2 ; 9,2.

[36] Cf. *Eph.* 1,1 ; 9,1 ; 14,1 (*bis*), 2 ; *Mag.* 1,2 ; 13,1 ; *Trall.* 8,1 ; *Philad.* 11,2 ; *Smyrn. init.* ; 1,1 ; 6,1 ; 13,2 ; *Pol.* 6,2. Cf. also *Mag.* 5,2 ; 6,1 ; *Philad.* 9,2. On the reading πίστιν καὶ ἀγάπην Ἰησοῦ Χριστοῦ in *Rom. init.* Cf. note 27 on page 77.

faith is your guide (ἀναγωγεύς), and love is the way that leads up to God »[37]. Again, he says that faith and love are « the beginning and end of life : faith is the beginning and love is the end »[38]. Faith and love are simply the two most prominent features of the Christian life. Faith is also associated with endurance (ὑπομονή)[39], long-suffering (μακροθυμία)[40], and concord (ὁμόνοια)[41]. The Pauline triad of faith, hope, and love is not found in the Ignatian Epistles[42].

The fundamental importance of faith is clearly recognized by Ignatius. « For the whole matter is faith and love, before which (ὧν) nothing has been preferred »[43]. It is even said that Christ was crucified on behalf of faith, i. e. that men might believe in him on account of his death[44]. Finally, the martyr bishop writes thus to Polycarp : « Please him under whose command you serve, from whom also you

---

[37] Cf. *Eph.* 9,1. Lightfoot and Lake translate ἀναγωγεύς by « windlass », understanding it to be a machine for drawing water ; and Sophocles (*Greek Lexicon of the Roman and Byzantine Periods*, *s. v.*) explains it as a rope. But when used in this connection, ἀναγωγεύς is neither the windlass nor the rope but the container for the water. Cf. Eustathius, *Opuscula* (ed. Tafel), p. 328. « Bucket » would be a better translation. However, the figure is not that of a machine for drawing water, but that of a guide to conduct one along a road. The Latin version is right in rendering the word by *dux*. Bauer translates it by « Geleiter nach oben ».

[38] Cf *Eph.* 14,1

[39] Cf. *Eph.* 3,1 ; Pol. 6,2. Cf. also *Mag.* 9,2 (ὑπομένειν).

[40] Cf. *Eph.* 3,1.

[41] Cf. *Eph.* 13,1 ; *Philad.* 11,2.

[42] In *Philad.* 11, 2 Ignatius uses πίστις and ἀγάπη in connection with ἐλπίζειν : ὁ κύριος Ἰησοῦς Χριστός, εἰς ὃν ἐπλίζουσιν (sc. the Christians in Ephesus and Smyrna) σαρκί, ψυχῇ, πνεύματι, πίστει, ἀγάπῃ, ὁμονοίᾳ.

[43] Cf. *Smyrn.* 6,1.

[44] Cf. *Eph.* 16,2. Cf. also *Eph.* 14,1 ; *Mag.* 1,2 ; *Philad.* 9,2.

receive your wages. Let no one of you be found a deserter. Let your baptism abide as weapons, faith as helmet, love as spear, endurance as full armour. »[45]

Faith is the distinguishing mark between Christians and other men. Those who have it are called « believers » (πιστοί)[46], and those who do not possess it are spoken of as « unbelievers » (ἄπιστοι)[47]. Heretics are also rated as « unbelievers », because their faith is partial or defective[48]. Moreover, a sharp distinction is made between faith and unbelief. So radically do they differ that it is impossible for one to do the works of the other[49]. There are two coinages — one of God and the other of the world; and, as one might expect, each bears its own impress. Believers have upon them the impress of God, and unbelievers that of the world[50].

Ignatius' conception of the Christian life is similar to that of Paul and the Fourth Evangelist. God or Christ, who is in truth God, dwells in the Christian, and consequently the latter is the temple of Christ or God[51]. It is not expressly said that this divine indwelling is mediated or brought

---

[45] Cf. *Pol.* 6,2.

[46] Cf. *Eph.* 21,2; *Mag.* 5,2; *Rom.* 3,2; *Smyrn.* 1,2. In the last-mentioned passage Lightfoot translates πιστούς by « faithful »; but it is better, with Lake and Bauer, to take it in the active sense. Only once does Ignatius use the adjective πιστός in the passive sense (*Trall.* 13,3), in which case it refers to God.

[47] Cf. *Mag.* 5,2.

[48] Cf. *Trall.* 10,1; *Smyrn.* 2,1; 5,3.

[49] Cf. *Eph.* 8,2.

[50] Cf. *Mag.* 5,2.

[51] Cf. *Eph.* 15,3 (κατοικεῖν, εἶναι ἐν ἡμῖν, ναός); *Mag.* 12 (Χριστὸν ἔχειν ἐν ἑαυτοῖς); 14 (θεοῦ γέμειν); *Rom.* 6,3 (θεὸν ἐν ἑαυτῷ ἔχειν); *Philad.* 7,2 (ναὸς θεοῦ). The Johannine μένειν is not used by Ignatius in this connection.

about by faith; but nevertheless to possess God or Christ in this way is the prerogative only of those who believe in Christ.

Ignatius, like Paul, thinks of faith as the sphere in which Christians should live. As they are in Christ, so they ought also to be in faith and love. Ignatius found the believers in Smyrna « equipped in immovable faith » and « established in love »[52]; and he bids those in Tralles to « rebuild » themselves « in faith, which is the flesh of the Lord, and in love, which is the blood of Jesus Christ »[53].

The results of faith in the lives of Christians are many and great. Indeed, since faith is primary and fundamental in Christianity, all the blessings of their religion are in reality ultimately due to their faith in Christ. Its power is manifest. The destruction wrought by Satan is brought to naught by the concord of faith[54]. No one who makes a genuine profession of faith commits sin[55]; for the nature of a tree is manifest from its fruit, and sin is not a product of faith. Finally, as God raised Christ from the dead, so will he also raise those who believe in him. Their faith insures their resurrection[56].

Ignatius speaks twice of being justified (δικαιοῦσθαι), i. e. approved by God[57]; but in neither case is faith the means whereby the divine approval is won. The Pauline doctrine that a believer in Christ is justified or acquitted

---

52 Cf. *Smyrn.* 1,1.
53 Cf. *Trall.* 8,1. Cf. also *Eph.* 20,1 and 2; *Mag.* 1,1; 6,1.
54 Cf. *Eph.* 13,1.
55 Cf. *Eph.* 14,2.
56 Cf. *Trall.* 9,2.
57 Cf. *Rom.* 5,1; *Philad.* 8,2.

by God on the basis of faith is not found in the Ignatian Epistles.

Salvation is understood in an eschatological way. It is the end and consummation of the Christian life, and it is dependent upon faith. The death of Christ on the cross, unintelligible and offensive to unbelievers, has made salvation and eternal life possible for those who believe in him [58]. Faith in Christ is the indispensable condition. It is indeed the beginning of life[59]. Even the ancient prophets, who hoped in him and awaited his coming, were saved in him by virtue of their faith [60]. On the other hand the heavenly powers and the angels will be condemned, « if they do not believe in the blood of Christ » [61].

In the Ignatian Epistles faith is primarily trust, and it includes self-surrender and loyalty. It is indeed the basic principle of the Christian life, which is understood in a thoroughly mystical way; but faith is not thought of as the source of moral excellence.

---

[58] Cf. *Eph.* 18,1; *Trall.* 2,1.

[59] Cf. *Eph.* 14,1.

[60] Cf. *Philad.* 5,2. The prepositional phrase ἐν ᾧ should be construed with ἐσώθησαν rather than πιστεύσαντες. It denotes the sphere in which the prophets' salvation was realized. Lake (*The Apostolic Fathers*, I., p. 243) thinks Ignatius probably means the Christian prophets; but there can be little doubt that he has in mind the Old Testament prophets. This is indicated by the language. Cf. Bauer in Lietzmann's *Handbuch zum Neuen Testament, Ergänzungsband*, II., pp. 225, 227, and 258. On the relation of the prophets to Christ cf. *Mag.* 9, 3.

[61] Cf. *Smyrn.* 6,1.

III. *Polycarp.*

Of the words relating to faith and believing only two are found in the Greek text of the Epistle of Polycarp, viz. πίστις and πιστεύειν. *Fides* and *credere* occur in the sections of the epistle which are extant only in Latin.

There can be no doubt that Polycarp had often read and pondered over the Epistles of Paul. Hence it is not surprising that faith should be frequently mentioned in his letter to the Philippians. The idea, however, is much less profound and distinctive than the Pauline conception of faith. It is only a part, though to be sure an essential part, of the Christian system.

The object of faith is usually Christ [62]. But in one case it is God, who raised him from the dead and gave him glory and a throne at God's right hand [63]; and in another passage both Christ and the Father are mentioned as the objects of Christian faith [64]. One could not believe in Christ without also believing in God.

Polycarp, like Paul, thought of faith as a divine gift, for he twice speaks of it as being given to Christians [65]. Nothing is said about the means employed to produce faith

[62] Πίστις and *fides* always denote faith in reference to Christ. The former is generally, and the latter is always, used absolutely. In *Polyc.* 1,3, however, πίστις takes an objective genitive. Πιστεύειν, when it signifies faith in God or Christ, is employed both absolutely (5,2) and with εἰς and the accusative (1,3; 2,1). The last two passages are reminiscences of 1 Pet. 1 : 8 and 1 : 21 respectively. In 12,2 *credere* is followed by *in* and the accusative.

[63] Cf. *Polyc.* 2,1.

[64] Cf. ibid. 12,2.

[65] Cf. ibid. 3,2; 4,2

or the part played by human agents in the process; but Polycarp must have believed that preachers and the Gospel message were necessary to bring men to the knowledge of Christ. Christians are the elect of God and Christ [66].

Faith is always subjective, — the fundamental religious attitude of trust. It is the state in which the followers of Christ must live [67], and they must be firm and immovable in it [68]. Faith is indeed the basic principle of the Christian life, and as such it is of prime importance. Hence Polycarp rejoices that « the steadfast root » of the Philippians' faith, « which is proclaimed from olden times, continues until now and bears fruit unto our Lord Jesus Christ » [69].

Moreover, faith is frequently mentioned in connection with those virtues which it is the duty of believers to cultivate, — love (ἀγάπη) [70], purity (ἁγνεία) [71], righteousness (δικαιοσύνη) [72], endurance (ὑπομονή) [73], long-suffering (*longanimitas* = μακροθυμία) [74], gentleness (*mansuetudo* = πραότης) [75], and edification (οἰκοδομή) [76]. It is also once associated with truth (*veritas* = ἀλήθεια) [77]. Faith, however, which is called « the mother of us all », occupies the first place. Hope « follows after » and love towards God and Christ and towards one's neighbour « goes

---

[66] Cf. ibid. 1,1.
[67] Cf. ibid. 4,2; 9,2.
[68] Cf. ibid. 10,1.
[69] Cf. ibid. 1,2.
[70] Cf. ibid. 4,2; 10,1.
[71] Cf. ibid. 4,2; 12,2.
[72] Cf. ibid. 9,2.
[73] Cf. ibid. 12,2; 13,2.
[74] Cf. ibid. 12,2.
[75] Cf. ibid. 10,1; 12,2.
[76] Cf. ibid. 13,2.
[77] Cf. ibid 12,2.

before ». It is said that « if anyone is within these, he has fulfilled the commandment of righteousness; for he who has love is far from all sin »[78].

Polycarp does not discuss the question of justification[79]. But in regard to salvation he has a clear and definite doctrine. It is based on the teaching of Paul, but in some respects it is different. According to the great Apostle to the Gentiles one is saved by grace and through faith[80]. The former operates through election in accordance with the divine will; and the latter is the means whereby the individual receives the Holy Spirit and comes into mystical fellowship with Christ, who is his hope of salvation[81]. Grace and faith working together produce salvation; works of the law are excluded. Polycarp also emphasizes God's part in the process, though he does not ignore the conditions to be fulfilled by man. He writes thus to the Philippians: « By grace you are saved, not of works, but by the will of God through Jesus Christ »[82]. Later he reminds them that « if we conduct ourselves worthily of him (i. e. Christ), we shall also reign with him, if indeed we have faith »[83]. According to Paul one is saved

---

[78] Cf. ibid. 3,2f. Cf. Rom. 13 : 8ff., where love is declared to be the fulfillment of the law.

[79] The verb δικαιοῦν is not used by Polycarp, and δικαιοσύνη always means 'righteousness' or 'moral excellence'.

[80] Cf. Eph. 2 : 8.

[81] Cf. Hatch, *The Pauline Idea of Faith*, p. 60.

[82] Cf. *Polyc.* 1,3. The first clause is quoted from Eph. 2 : 8, where διὰ πίστεως follows immediately after σεσωσμένοι. It is significant that Polycarp stops short at σεσωσμένοι, taking up the quotation again with οὐκ ἐξ ἔργων. By ἔργα he means, like the author of James, simply good conduct in general.

[83] Cf. ibid. 5,2.

by grace and faith, the latter being the source of moral excellence; according to Polycarp faith must be accompanied by good conduct, which is a product of the individual's will.

IV. *Didaché.*

The Didaché has very little to offer on the subject of faith. Nothing is said about its beginning, its working, or its end. However, the substantive πίστις occurs three times. No object is expressed, but in each case πίστις denotes Christian faith in the subjective sense. None of the other words which we are studying is found in the Didaché.

Faith is so important and fundamental in Christianity that the writer speaks of the period during which the readers have been Christians as « the whole time of your faith » [84]. It is faith that differentiates their present from their former life, and it is doubtless a mere accident that they are not called « believers ».

Faith is once conjoined with knowledge, as it is in the Fourth Gospel [85]; but the relation between them is not defined or discussöed. They are mentioned, along with immortality, as prominent Christian blessings, for which the believer should be grateful to God; and they are apparently regarded as coördinate. Faith is unterstood to be primarily intellectual. It is belief rather than trust, and hence it is naturally associated with knowledge. It is not a divine gift, but a free act on the part of the individual.

The Didaché opens with a discussion of the Two Ways, one leading to life and the other leading to death. The former

[84] Cf. ibid. 16,2.
[85] Cf. *Did.* 10,2.

is the way of Christian morality, which is based upon Jesus' summary of the law, certain passages from the Sermon on the Mount, and the second table of the Decalogue. Love, purity, truthfulness, and other social virtues are inculcated in this part of the work. These ought all to be cultivated by Christians, but none of them is brought into relation with faith. The latter is not thought of as the root from which moral excellence springs.

Justification is not mentioned in the Didaché. But as regards salvation we read as follows: « Then the creation of men will come into the burning of testing, and many will be offended and perish; but those who endure in their faith will be saved by the curse itself »[86]. In other words, salvation depends not upon faith, but upon endurance or steadfastness in faith, i. e. upon fidelity to Christ. The writer of the passage just quoted is contemplating the trials of the last days. To fall away from faith is to perish, but to be steadfast in it is to obtain salvation.

V. *Barnabas.*

Πίστις, πιστεύειν, and πιστός are the only words relating to faith or belief in the Epistle of Barnabas. The three negative words happen not to occur. The object, which is sometimes God[87] and sometimes Christ[88], is usually left

---

[86] Cf. ibid. 16,5. Ἐν πίστει is most naturally taken with ὑπομείναντες, though it is possible to connect it with σωθήσονται. Cf. Knopf in Lietzmann's *Handbuch zum N. T., Ergänzungsband*, I., p. 39.

[87] Cf. *Barn.* 13,7; 16,7. In 13,7 all the editors read θεῷ (א C) rather than κυρίῳ (G L). Abraham, by virtue of his faith or trust in Jahveh, is « the father of the nations which believe in God in uncircumcision ».

[88] Cf. ibid. 4,8; 6,3. In the latter passage ὁ πιστεύων εἰς (א CL) is better supported than ὃς ἐλπίσει ἐπ' (G), and should

to be inferred from the context; but in some cases it is expressed [89].

Πίστις in Barnabas usually means 'faith'. It is fundamentally trust in God or Christ, and it contains no trace of mysticism. The intellectual element in the idea is secondary. Faith or trust is of primary importance in Barnabas's conception of Christianity.

Faith arises from the hearing of the Gospel [90]. The missionaries preach the word, and some of their hearers believe in Christ and become his followers. Barnabas, however, unlike Paul, does not regard faith as a divine gift. It results from an exercice of will on the part of the individual, though God foresaw « that people whom he had prepared in his Beloved, would believe in guilelessness » [91]. According to the printed editions, Barnabas speaks of the period in which Christians have been believers in Christ as « the whole time of their faith », or « the whole time of their life and faith » [92].

---

probably be preferred. Some scholars think ὁ πιστεύων εἰς was introduced from the LXX (Is. 28 : 16). However, the preposition εἰς is not attested in this place. The following *variae lectiones* occur in Is. 28 : 16 ὁ πιστεύων, like the Hebrew, (B ed. Vat. text); ὁ πιστεύων ἐπ' αὐτῷ (א AQ); ὁ πιστεύων ἐν αὐτῷ (ed. Vat. marg.). In *Barn.* 6,3 Funk reads ὁ πιστεύων εἰς; whereas Gebhardt-Harnack, Lightfoot, and Lake have adopted ὃς ἐλπίσει ἐπ'.

89 Πίστις takes an objective genitive twice (4,8; 6, 17). In the former case the object is Christ, and in the latter it is the divine promise. Πιστεύειν, when it is used of God and the object is expressed, governs the dative (13,7; 16,7). In 6,3, according to א CL, the prepositional phrase εἰς αὐτόν, referring to Christ, is found with the participle πιστεύων.

90 Cf. ibid. 9,3; 11,11.

91 Cf. ibid. 3,6.

92 Cf. ibid. 4,9. Cf. *Did.* 16,2 : οὐ γὰρ ὠφελήσει ὑμᾶς ὁ πᾶς χρόνος τῆς πίστεως ὑμῶν. The following *variae lectiones* are found in *Barn.*

Faith, however, is not thought of as the state or sphere in which they live.

Barnabas, like Paul, associates hope and love with faith [93]; and he also resembles the Apostle to the Gentiles in holding that hope springs from faith in Christ [94]. But this is neither said nor implied in the case of love. Similarly, certain other Christian virtues are mentioned in connection with faith; but they are not regarded as resulting from it, though faith is primary. « The aids of our faith are fear (φόβος) and endurance (ὑπομονή), and our allies are longsuffering (μακροθυμία) and self-control (ἐγκράτεια) [95].

Barnabas's purpose in writing his epistle was that his readers, along with their faith, might have their knowledge perfect [96]. Christians should be equipped with mature faith

---

4,9: τῆς πίστεως ὑμῶν ℵ; τῆς ζωῆς ἡμῶν C; *vitae nostrae et fidei* L. It is possible that C preserves the original text, and that πίστεως was substitued for ζωῆς through the influence of *Did.*16,2 (ℵ). Then L would represent a combination of the readings attested by ℵ and C. For a different explanation cf. Windisch in *op. cit.*, p. 324. Lightfoot, Gebhardt-Harnack, and Lake adopt τῆς πίστεως ἡμῶν, whereas Funk reads τῆς ζωῆς καὶ πίστεως ἡμῶν. The phrase *omne fidei tempus* in a somewhat different sense occurs in the Latin version of Irenaeus (*Adv. Haer.* II., 22,2).

[93] Cf. ibid. 1,4; 11,8.

[94] Cf. ibid. 4,8. Πίστεως in the phrase ἐν ἐλπίδι τῆς πίστεως αὐτοῦ is a subjective genitive. In 1,6 the « hope of life » is declared to be « the beginning and end of our faith ». Πίστεως, which is attested by C, is omitted by ℵ L; but it is required by the sense, and is doubtless a true part of the sentence. Nevertheless, § 6 is clearly not in harmony with the context, and should probably be regarded as a gloss or interpolation. Cf. Windisch in Lietzmann's *Handbuch zum N. T., Ergänzungsband*, III., pp. 305 f.

[95] Cf. ibid. 2,2.

[96] Cf. ibid. 1,5.

and perfect knowledge. The writer probably thought of knowledge as coming after faith and confirming it — a view which led later to the Gnostics' exaltation of knowledge at the expense of faith.

Justification in the theological sense is mentioned only once in the Epistle of Barnabas [97], and then nothing is said about the means by which one is justified. On the other hand, salvation, which is conceived in an eschatological way, is a prominent and frequently recurring idea in the work. The Son of God came in the flesh and suffered on our account (δι' ἡμᾶς), « that his smiting might make us alive » [98]. This was prefigured by the healing of the Israelites who resorted to the brazen serpent « put upon the tree » in the wilderness [99]. But in order that the individual may gain the benefit of Christ's redemptive work, faith is necessary on his part. « He who believes in him shall live for ever » [100]. However, faith alone is not enough to insure salvation.

[97] Cf. ibid. 6,1. Ὁ δικαιούμενός μοι means 'he who would justify himself before me' (Windisch), not 'he that goeth to law with Me' (Lightfoot) or 'he that seeks justice against me' (Lake). The participle is conative. Barnabas is quoting Is. 50 : 8 from memory. All manuscripts of the LXX have ὁ κρινόμενός μοι here. Irenaeus, however, (*Adv. Haer.* IV 33,13) has *quisquis iustificatur* (the Greek text is lost). Cf. also *Apost. Preach,* 88. The Vulgate renders the Hebrew correctly (מי בעל משפטי = *quis est adversarius meus*). In 4,10 and 15,7 δικαιοῦν signifies 'to make righteous', not 'to acquit'.

[98] Cf. ibid. 5,10 ; 7,2.

[99] Cf. ibid. 12,7.

[100] Cf. ibid. 6,3. Cf. above, p. 87, note 88. In 11,11 the passage « Whosoever shall eat from these (i. e. the beautiful trees just mentioned), shall live for ever » is explained as meaning « whosoever shall hear these things spoken and believe, shall live for ever ». The passage quoted is a medley of Scriptural reminiscences (Ezek. 47 : 1-12 ; Gen. 3 : 6, 22 ; Dan. 7 : 10 LXX ; John 6 : 51).

« For the whole time of our life and faith will profit us nothing, if we do not now in the lawless season and the coming offences resist, as becomes the sons of God, that the Black One may not get a chance to slip in »[101]. One must also « flee altogether from all the works of lawlessness », and one must « hate the error of the present time », which is sin in various forms[102]. In other words, moral effort as well as faith is required for salvation.

Πίστις is always subjective in the Epistle of Barnabas. It is nowhere used objectively to denote « the faith », i. e. the substance or content of Christian teaching.

The adjective πιστός, which occurs only twice, has the passive sense in both instances. In one case it means 'faithful'[103], and in the other 'trustworthy' or 'sure'[104].

VI. *Hermas.*

Hermas uses only four of the words which we are investigating: πίστις, πιστεύειν, πιστός, and ἀπιστία[105]. The latter is employed as a proper name and occurs but once[106], whilst πίστις and πιστεύειν greatly predominate over πιστός.

---

[101] Cf. ibid. 4,9. I have followed, though not without misgiving, the text of Funk. Lightfoot, Gebhardt-Harnack, and Lake omit τῆς ζωῆς καί. Cf. above p. 88 note 92.

[102] Cf. ibid. 4,1.

[103] Cf. ibid. 21,4.

[104] Cf. ibid. 11,5 (= Is. 33 : 16 LXX).

[105] *Incredibilis*, presumably representing ἄπιστον of the Greek original and meaning 'incredible', is found once in the concluding portion of the Shepherd (*Sim.* 9. 31,6), which is extant only in Latin and Ethiopic. The latter version also implies ἄπιστον in the above-mentioned passage.

[106] Cf. *Sim.* 9. 15,3. Ἀπιστία is the first of the four more powerful women clad in black garments and corresponds to Πίστις

Faith is frequently mentioned by Hermas. But he is in no sense a theologian, and he has no doctrine of faith. It is simply a common Christian concept, an essential element in Christianity as he knew it. He does not attempt to analyze it or to assign it a place in a system of thought. His purpose in writing the Shepherd was eminently practical, and his theme is repentance and moral living.

Nevertheless, faith has real religious value in the Shepherd of Hermas. Sometimes the intellectual element in it predominates, and it means 'belief'; but in most cases it is simply trust. Belief in God as the sole creator and artificer of the universe is primary and fundamental[107], but such belief is only the beginning. Belief which is not based upon investigation or inquiry is of little worth[108]. To belief one must add faith, or trust, which is the right attitude of mind and heart towards the Deity. This is indispensable for the religious life.

Faith is often mentioned in connection with certain other ideas, — e. g. love (ἀγάπη)[109], righteousness (δικαιοσύνη)[110], virtue (ἀρετή)[111], and truth (ἀλήθεια)[112]. All of these have moral and religious value, and they are characteristic of the Christian ideal of life. The nature of faith is clearly indicated by being contrasted with doubtful-mindedness

---

in the preceding section. The latter is the first of the four more powerful virgins, who stand at the corners of the Tower. In *Vis.* 3. 8,2 ff. Πίστις is the name given to the first of the seven women who support the Tower. She is the mother of Ἐγκράτεια.

[107] Cf. *Man.* 1.1.

[108] Cf. *Man.* 10.1, 4.

[109] Cf. *Man.* 8.9; *Sim.* 9.17,4; 9.18,4.

[110] Cf. *Man.* 8.9; 12.3,1.

[111] Cf. *Man.* 12.3,1.

[112] Cf. *Man.* 8.9; 12.3,1.

(διψυχία). Faith or trust is diametrically opposed to this and has the opposite effect in practice. Doubtful-mindedness is a wrong relation towards God. It prevents one from receiving an answer to one's petitions [113]; and when danger arises and divine help is needed, it leads to disaster [114].

In the great majority of cases the object of faith is not expressed. In some instances, however, the object is specified, — God [115], Christ [116], or the divine Spirit, i. e. the Spirit of God [117]. Hermas does not regard faith as the means of bringing the individual into mystical fellowship with the Deity. He is an excellent representative of the moralism or nomism of second century Christianity, and the mystical aspect of religion is quite foreign to his mind.

Hermas holds that faith is of divine origin. « You see then, says he (i. e. the shepherd), that faith is from above

---

[113] Cf. *Man.* 9.7. Cf. also Jas. 1 : 6 ff.; *Man.* 9. 6, 9, 10, 12; *Sim.* 6. 1, 2.

[114] Cf. *Vis.* 4. 2, 4. Cf. also *Vis.* 3. 7, 1; 4. 2, 6.

[115] For πίστις with an objective genitive cf. *Vis.* 4. 1,8; *Man.* 11.4; *Sim.* 6. 1,2; 6. 3,6. For πιστεύειν with the dative cf. *Vis.* 4. 2,6; *Man.* 1.2; 9.7; 12. 6,2; *Sim.* 5. 1,5; 9. 13,5.

[116] For πίστις with an objective genitive cf. *Sim.* 9. 16,5. For πιστεύειν with εἰς and the accusative cf. *Man.* 4. 3,3; *Sim.* 8. 3,2. It is worthy of note that when πιστεύειν denotes faith or belief in Christ, the object is expressed by means of εἰς and the accusative. In *Sim.* 9. 17,4 ἐπὶ τῷ ὀνόματι should be taken with ἐκλήθησαν. So Lipsius, Zahn, Gebhardt-Harnack, Lightfoot, Lake, Dibelius, and the Old Latin translation (ed. Hilgenfeld). The Palatine version, on the other hand, has *crediderunt in nomen filii dei*, with nothing to represent ἐκλήθησαν.

[117] For πίστις with an objective genitive cf. *Man.* 11.9. For πιστεύειν with the dative cf. 11.17 and 21. In *Sim.* 9. 1,1 the Holy Spirit (τὸ πνεῦμα τὸ ἅγιον) is identified with « the Son of God ». Cf. Dibelius in Lietzmann's *Handbuch zum N. T., Ergänzungsband,* IV., p. 602. Cf. 2 Cor. 3 : 17.

from the Lord and has great power »[118]. However, faith in Christ arose from hearing the Gospel preached[119]. The missionaries proclaimed the message, and some of their hearers believed. These « received the seal», i. e. were baptized, on the strength of their faith and became Christians[120]. Faith precedes baptism as its necessary condition, and baptism normally follows faith.

Hermas speaks several times of « the elect of God » or « the elect of the Lord », and in one passage he says that they are saved through faith[121]. So, too, some have been called through Christ, or by Christ, to salvation[122]. These are of course those who have believed, though nothing is said about their faith. Believers are the elect and the called.

Faith is so essential to the Christian life that it is often thought of as the sphere in which Christians live[123]. It is not, however, a mystical state, for Hermas is in no sense a mystic. « Those who are complete in faith ask all things, trusting in the Lord, and receive them »[124]. So, too, « as many as are full in faith, resist him (i. e. the devil) mightily, and he departs from them, not having a place where he may

118 Cf. *Man.* 9.11.

119 Cf. *Sim.* 8. 3,2 ; 9. 17,4.

120 Cf. *Sim.* 8. 6,3. According to *Sim.* 9. 16,5 the dead in Hades heard the preaching of the Apostles and other Christian teachers and received from them « the seal of the preaching », i. e. baptism. Belief is of course presupposed. Even the righteous of pre-Christian times cannot obtain salvation without baptism. Cf. *Sim.* 9. 16,2 and 3. Cf. also [Mk.] 16 : 16, where baptism is implied in the second clause.

121 Cf. *Vis.* 3. 8,3.

122 Cf. *Sim.* 8. 11,1 ; 9. 14,5.

123 Cf. *Vis.* 3. 5,4 and 5,5 ; 3. 12,3 ; *Man.* 5. 2,1 ; 12. 6,1 ; *Sim.* 8. 9,1 ; 9. 23,2.

124 Cf. *Man.* 9. 6,

enter in »[125]. Moreover, it is said that the Apostles and teachers who preached the name of Christ fell asleep « in the power and faith of the Son of God »[126]. The author of the Shepherd also contrasts faith as the essence of Christianity with the mere name. « Such men have a name indeed, but they are void of faith, and there is no fruit of truth in them »[127]. These and many other passages testify to the fundamental importance of faith in Christianity.

Christians must hold fast to faith as a permanent possession. They must abide in it and work its works, that is, they must do only those things which are consonant with it[128]. To fall from faith or to renounce it, unless one repents in time, will inevitably lead to ultimate rejection and condemnation.

Hermas has much to say on the subject of morals, which he treats from the point of view of moralism or nomism. He exhorts his readers to shun sin, and to keep the commandments of God, that they may « live ». Faith should be accompanied by good works[129]. But the righteous acts of believers are not thought of as resulting from faith. The individual is entirely free. He must choose what is right and do it.

Hermas mentions many virtues in the Shepherd. Some of them are general, like righteousness (δικαιοσύνη), and others are specific, like purity (ἁγνεία) and longsuffering (μακροθυμία). Two passages, however, deserve special consideration. In each of them the writer gives a list of outstanding Christian

---

125 Cf. *Man.* 12. 5,4.
126 Cf. *Sim.* 9. 16,5.
127 Cf. *Sim.* 9. 19,2. Cf. also *Vis.* 3. 6,5.
128 Cf. *Sim.* 8. 9,1.
129 Cf. *Sim.* 8. 10,3.

virtues in personified form, and in the second case he enumerates an equal number of vices [130]. (1) The Tower is supported by seven women, whose names are these: Faith (Πίστις), Self-control (Ἐγκράτεια), Simplicity (Ἁπλότης), Guilelessness (Ἀκακία), Gravity (Σεμνότης), Knowledge (Ἐπιστήμη), and Love (Ἀγάπη) [131]. (2) Twelve virgins stand about the Tower, and these are their names: Faith (Πίστις), Self-control (Ἐγκράτεια), Power (Δύναμις), Longsuffering (Μακροθυμία), Simplicity (Ἁπλότης), Guilelessness (Ἀκακία), Purity (Ἁγνεία), Cheerfulness (Ἱλαρότης), Truth (Ἀλήθεια), Understanding (Σύνεσις), Concord (Ὁμόνοια), and Love (Ἀγάπη) [132]. It is worthy of note that both of these lists begin with Faith and end with Love, and that Hope, the other member of the Pauline triad, does not appear in either of them. In the former passage Self-control is called the daughter of Faith, and the other virtues are said to be daughters one of the other. But these relationships are in fact merely a part of the allegory and have no real significance. The writer does not mean that self-control springs from faith.

Justification in the theological sense and sanctification are each mentioned once in the Shepherd [133]. Neither of them, however, is connected with faith, though the writer is speaking of Christians. « Keep this thy flesh pure and undefiled,

---

130 For a list of personified virtues, which are described as sisters, see Cebes *Tab.* 20,3.

131 Cf. *Vis.* 3. 8,3 ff. I have followed, with Dibelius, the order of AL [1], which is vindicated by § 7. In L[2] and Clem. Alex. (*Strom.* II. 55,3) Ἐπιστήμη follows Ἁπλότης. The Ethiopic version reads thus: *Innocentia, Hilaritas, Caritas, Castitas, Sinceritas.*

132 Cf. *Sim.* 9.15,2.

133 Cf. *Vis.* 3. 9,1; *Sim.* 5. 7,1. Δικαιοῦν in *Vis.* 3. 9,1 and *Man.* 5. 1,7 means 'to make righteous', not 'to justify', i. e. to account righteous or acquit at the bar of God.

that the spirit which dwells in it may bear witness to it, and thy flesh may be justified », i. e. acquitted or accounted righteous at the final judgment [134]. This may be called justification by clean living, which is a form of justification by works. The good works by which a man is justified according to James are positive and social, whereas the goodness or virtue contemplated in the passage before us is individual and negative. Hermas is remote in time and spirit from the Pauline controversy over justification, and he gives no evidence that the question ever occurred to him.

Πίστις in the Shepherd of Hermas always means 'faith' in the subjective sense. It is, as has been said above, fundamentally either trust or belief. The word is nowhere used to denote the substance or content of Christian teaching [135].

The adjective πιστός usually has the active meaning. Faith is the most distinctive feature of the Christian life,

---

[134] Cf. *Sim*. 5. 7,1. The indwelling spirit is not the Holy Spirit, which according to Paul dwells in all Christians and makes them 'pneumatic'. It is rather the good spirit which God has caused to dwell in the flesh (cf. *Man*. 3.1). This idea has been Christianized in certain respects. Cf. Dibelius in *op. cit.*, IV., pp. 517 ff. It is worthy of note that Hermas always uses κατοικεῖν and κατοικίζειν in this connection. To denote the indwelling of the divine (God, Christ, or the Holy Spirit) Paul employs οἰκεῖν (Rom. 8 : 9,11 ; 1 Cor. 3 : 16), ἐνοικεῖν (Rom. 8 : 11 ; 2 Cor. 6 : 16 ; cf. also 2 Tim. 1 : 14), and κατοικεῖν (Eph. 3 : 17) without any appreciable difference in meaning. The Johannine word is μένειν. Cf. above p. 42, note 23 ; p. 48, note 53. Cf. also Hatch, *op. cit.*, p. 41, note 1, and p. 44, note 5.

[135] Πίστις may have the objective sense in *Man*. 8.10 (ἐσκανδαλισμένους ἀπὸ τῆς πίστεως μὴ ἀποβάλλεσθαι). However, the word is here susceptible of the subjective meaning ; and since this accords with the usage of Hermas, it should probably be adopted in this passage.

and hence Christians are spoken of as « believing » [136]. However the word is also found in the passive sense, meaning either 'faithful' [137] or 'credible' [138].

VII. *The Second Epistle of Clement.*

The homily commonly known as Second Clement is theologically unlike any of the writings of the New Testament [139]. All the words which we are studying are found in it except ἀπιστεῖν. Nevertheless, in spite of the thoroughly Christian character of the work, faith plays a very small part in the writer's thought. He is primarily a moralist, and his main object is to induce his readers to lead an upright life. He teaches that by repentance and good conduct they can obtain eternal life [140]. Salvation is not said to be dependent upon faith; but it must be borne in mind that the homily is addressed to believers in Christ, who saved them when they were perishing [141]. Naturally in a writing of this sort the idea of justification does not appear.

---

[136] Cf. *Vis.* 3. 5,4; *Man.* 4. 1,4; 6. 2,7; 9.9; 11.1 (*bis*); *Sim.* 8. 7, 4; 8. 9,1; 8. 10,1; 9. 22,1. In *Man.* 6. 2,7 Gebhardt and Harnack have adopted πιστότατος on the authority of Simonides's copy of the Athos manuscript and what seems to have been the reading of L¹; whereas Lightfoot, Funk, and Lake read πιστός (L² Eth). In this case the notorious Simonides was right in reporting the reading of A. Πιστότατος (AL¹), meaning 'very strong in faith', should probably be accepted as the correct reading.

[137] Cf. *Sim.* 5. 2,2.

[138] Cf. *Man.* 3.5 (*bis*).

[139] Cf. Gebhardt, Harnack, and Zahn, *Patrum Apostolicorum Opera* ², I., 1, p. LXX.

[140] Cf. 2 Clem. 5,6; 8,2,4,6; 11,7; 13,1; 15,1; 17,1; 19,1, 3 f.

[141] Cf. ibid. 1,4.

The theme of Second Clement is general moral uprightness rather than any particular virtues. However, love [142], peace [143], self-control [144], and endurance [145] are mentioned; but the writer does not think of these or of moral excellence in general as resulting from faith. A Christian is under obligation to live an upright life, and love, peace, self-control, and endurance are merely some of the virtues which he ought to cultivate. Nevertheless, it is recognized that Christian faith, with its promise of future blessedness, enables one to bear up under the trials of life [146].

Christians are a separate people, differing alike from Jews and pagans; and it is their faith in Christ that makes the difference. Before they believed in him, they « seemed to be forsaken of God »; but since they believed, they have become more numerous than « those who seem to have God », i. e. the Jews [147].

In the only passage of Second Clement in which the substantive πίστις occurs it is associated with love (ἀγάπη), and the two together seem simply to denote the right attitude of mind and heart for a Christian to have [148]. Faith and love are primary characteristics of the Christian consciousness, and every believer in Christ should have them. No object

---

[142] Cf. ibid. 4,3; 9,6; 12,1; 16,4.

[143] Cf. ibid. 10,2.

[144] Cf. ibid. 15,1.

[145] Cf. ibid. 11,5; 17,7.

[146] Cf. ibid. 20,2. In this passage the writer discusses in a practical way the main problem of theodicy: Why do the wicked flourish and the righteous suffer?

[147] Cf. ibid. 2,3.

[148] Cf. ibid. 15,2. Knopf (in Lietzmann's *Handbuch zum N. T.*, *Ergänzungsband*, I., p. 175) explains πίστεως as mutual trust on the part of the speaker and the hearer.

is expressed, and probably none was consciously present to the writer's mind.

On the other hand unbelief (ἀπιστία) is the enemy of the Christian life. « For sometimes when we do evil things, we do not know it on account of the doublemindedness and unbelief which is in our breasts » [149]. «Unbelief» here is neither refusal to accept Christ after the manner of Jews and pagans nor the utter rejection of him which constituted apostasy. It is rather the dullness or lukewarmness of faith that at times assails believers and makes them morally and spiritually half-dead. If the Christian life is to flourish as it should, faith must be sound and strong. In like manner Christians whose faith has become weak and ineffectual are spoken of as « the unbelievers » (οἱ ἄπιστοι) [150]. The word is not used of non-Christians, nor are Christians referred to as « believers » (πιστοί) [151].

If the author of Second Clement had been combatting false doctrine, he would probably have employed πίστις and πιστεύειν in the sense of 'belief' and 'believe' respectively; and he might, like the redactor of the Pastoral Epistles and the author of Jude, have designated orthodoxy by the brief and convenient term « the faith ». But no emphasis is laid upon the intellectual side of Christianity. Faith is not associated with knowledge [152]. The problem that confronts the writer

---

[149] Cf. ibid. 19,2.

[150] Cf. ibid. 17,5.

[151] The adjective πιστός is used three times in Second Clement (8,5 *bis*; 11,6). In each case it occurs in a quotation from the New Testament and means 'faithful'.

[152] In 17,5 εἰδέναι and πιστεύειν are used together; but πιστεύειν means 'to be convinced' or 'to accept as true', not 'to have faith' in reference to God or Christ.

is how to improve the moral and spiritual conditions of the Christians whom he is addressing. Nevertheless, if he had thought of faith as Paul did, making it the basic principle of both religion and ethics, he would certainly have made more use of it than he does.

VIII. *The Martyrdom of Polycarp.*

In the so-called Martyrdom of Polycarp, a circular letter written in the name of the church in Smyrna and describing the martyrdom of the venerable Polycarp, the adjectives πιστός and ἄπιστος are the only words which relate to faith or belief. They are both used in the active sense and as technical terms. Πιστός denotes Christians as believers in Christ[153]; and those who do not believe in him, whether pagans or Jews, are called ἄπιστοι[154]. In other words faith or belief in Christ is felt to be the distinguishing mark of a Christian. It is a mere accident that the verb πιστεύειν is not employed.

Love[155] and joy[156] are mentioned in the epistle, and much stress is naturally laid upon endurance[157]; but none of these characteristic marks of the Christian life is brought into relation with faith. According to Paul these and other Christian virtues result directly or indirectly from faith[158].

---

153 Cf. *Mart. Polyc.* 12,3; 13,2.

154 Cf. ibid. 16,1.

155 Cf. ibid. 1,2. In the salutation the author prays that « the mercy and peace and love of God the Father and our Lord Jesus Christ » may be multiplied.

156 Cf. ibid. 12,1; 18,2.

157 Cf. ibid. 3,1; 19,2. Cf. also 2,2,3,4; 13,3.

158 Cf. Hatch, *op. cit.* pp. 51 ff.

Knowledge (ἐπίγνωσις) of God has been received through Christ [159]; but such knowledge is neither mediated through faith nor associated with it. So, too, Christ « suffered for the salvation of the whole world of those who are saved »[160]; but salvation is not expressly connected with faith. The latter does not appear as the condition on which one is saved, or as the means by which one obtains eternal life. Nevertheless only believers in Christ can participate in the salvation wrought by him.

Believers are the elect [161]. Their faith makes it evident that God has elected them to salvation. Nothing is said about perseverance in faith, but it is unthinkable that anyone who has lost his faith or apostatized should be numbered among the saved.

It is somewhat surprising that the author of the Martyrdom of Polycarp does not even once mention faith. But it must be remembered that he was writing an account of a martyr's death, and not a theological treatise. However, he does not seem to have grasped the fundamental significance of faith in Christianity.

---

159 Cf. *Mart. Polyc.* 14,1.

160 Cf. ibid. 17,2.

161 Cf. ibid. 16,1. Τῶν ἐκλεκτῶν, standing in contrast to τῶν ἀπίστων, is practically equivalent to τῶν πιστῶν.

Chapter VI.

THE GREEK APOLOGISTS.

I. *Aristides.*

None of the words which we are studying occurs in either of the papyrus fragments of Aristides or in the Greek text embedded in the romance of Barlaam and Josaphat [1]. The Armenian version contains the substantive corresponding to πίστις, and the Syriac translation has the verbs *haimen* and *shar*.

[1] With the exception of two papyrus fragments recently discovered in Egypt (cf. *The Oxyrhynchus Papyri*, XV., pp. 1 ff.; and *The Journal of Theological* Studies, XXV., pp. 73 ff.), the Greek original of Aristides's Apology is lost. But in a somewhat abbreviated and altered form the work is contained in the romance of Barlaam and Josaphat, which is ascribed to John of Damascus (cf. *Texts and Studies*, I., 1, pp. 100 ff.). The apology is extant in Syriac (cf. ibid., I., 1, *ad fin.*), and a fragment of an Armenian version has also been preserved (cf. Patres Mechitaristæ, *Sancti Aristidis Philosophi Atheniensis Sermones Duo*; Pitra, *Analecta Sacra*, iv.,) A comparison of the papyrus fragments with the Syriac version leads to the conclusion that the latter, in spite of its verbosity, in places reproduces the original more faithfully than the Greek text found in the story of Barlaam and Josaphat, « retaining words and phrases which the Greek redactor discarded. The latter often preserves the language of Aristides with much fidelity, but he treats the original with some freedom, making such short cuts and readjustments as seemed suitable for his purpose, and not confining himself to 'necessary modifications' ». (cf. *The Oxyrhynchus Papyri*, XV., pp. 2 f.). For what may possibly be a small fragment of an epistle of Aristides see *Texts and Studies*, I., 1, pp. 33 ff.

According to the Armenian version Aristides says: « By faith alone I glorify and adore him (i. e. God) »[2]. Faith is here contrasted with a full comprehension of the Deity[3], which transcends the powers of the human intellect. Faith or trust is the attitude of mind and heart which makes it possible for one to draw near to God in worship. The writer means that by faith alone he has been enabled, by the grace of God, to know him at least in part and to speak wisely concerning him.

In the Syriac translation the verb *haimen* means 'to believe in' three times, and the object of belief in each case is personal or quasi-personal — God, the gods of the Greeks, or « a nature which is invisible and all-seeing »[4]. In these passages the verb denotes a conviction that the being or beings mentioned exist, and its content is purely intellectual. Belief

---

[2] Cf. Patres Mechitaristae, *op. cit.*, p. 8 (translation on p. 9); Pitra, *op. cit.*, p. 7 (translation on p. 283). Von Himpel omits this clause in his German version (*Texte und Untersuchungen*, I., 1 and 2, pp. 110 ff.) apparently by inadvertence; but it is in the French translation of L. G. (*Revue de théologie et de philosophie*, XII., pp. 79 ff.) and also in the rendering of the Edschmiazin manuscript by Dr. Conybeare (*Texts and Studies*, I., 1, pp. 30 ff.).

[3] The following precedes the sentence just quoted: « Et pro meis viribus locutus sum, quin tamen altitudinem imperscrutabilis magnitudinis eius comprehendere possem ».

[4] Cf. *Texts and Studies*. I., 1, *ad fin.*, p. 11, 5 f. (in *Barlaam and Josaphat* VIII those who believe in the gods are referred to simply as αὐτοί); p. 21, 18 f. (in *Barlaam and Josaphat* XIII nothing is said about «a nature which is invisible and all-seeing»); p. 23, 11 (in *Barlaam and Josaphat* XV γινώσκουσι corresponds to *iāɣīn umhaimnīn* of the Syriac version). In each instance the object is introduced by the preposition *b*. *Shar* and *haimen* meaning 'to put credence in' take *l* with the object.

of this sort may be the basis of religion, but it is not in itself religious. The writer is not thinking of the trust or confidence which a religious man feels in God or in divine powers.

II. *Justin Martyr.*

Faith plays an important part in Justin Martyr's conception of Christianity; and, as one might expect in so voluminous a writer, he uses all the words which we are studying. His chief object in writing is to persuade his readers to believe in Christ.

Faith, as Justin understands it, is primarily belief rather than trust; and its object, which is often unexpressed, is usually Christ [5], though in some cases it is God [6]. One must

---

[5] Justin employs both πίστις and πιστεύειν to denote faith or belief in Christ. The substantive takes an objective genitive twice (*Dial.* 52,4; 111,2) and a prepositional phrase introduced by εἰς once (*Dial.* 40,1). In *Dial.* 121,2 Justin uses πρός with the accusative to express the object of πίστις, which is here religious faith directed towards the sun. He declares that no one ever endured death « on account of faith towards the sun ». In this respect sun-worship stands in striking contrast to Christianity. The object of πίστις, however, is usually unexpressed, being easily understood from the context. The verb πιστεύειν takes the dative 12 times, εἰς with the accusative 16 times, and ἐπί with the accusative 16 times. Πιστεύειν τινί properly means 'to believe' or 'put credence in someone'; whereas πιστεύειν εἰς Χριστόν and πιστεύειν ἐπὶ Χριστόν respectively denote faith or belief as directed towards Christ and as resting upon Christ. In practice, however, these distinctions are ignored by Justin, the three constructions being used interchangeably.

[6] Πίστις denotes faith in God once (*Apol.* I. 13,2), the object being expressed by the preposition ἐν with the dative. Πιστεύειν is

believe certain things concerning Christ, especially the Old Testament prophecies which were thought to refer to him; and one must also accept him as the Messiah. However, belief in Jesus as the Messiah implies trust and loyalty.

This is well illustrated by the Old Testament story of Abraham's colloquy with God, to which reference is made several times in the *Dialogue with Trypho*. When God promised the patriarch that he should have a son and heir, the latter « trusted in Jahveh »[7], having full and implicit confidence that the divine promise would be fulfilled. By means of his trust he was brought into a right relation with God. Justin, however, using the Septuagint, misses the meaning of the passage. He understands it in the sense that Abraham believed, or put credence in, what Jahveh had just said to him. « He believed the voice of God, and it was reckoned to him for righteousness »[8]. Hence when Justin speaks of Abraham's faith, he means belief rather than trust[9].

used this way six times. Twice it takes the dative (*Apol.* I. 18,6; *Dial.* 133,6), three times εἰς with the accusative (*Dial.* 30,2 *bis*; 116,3), and once ἐπί with the accusative (*Dial.* 83,4).

[7] Cf. Gen. 15 : 6 (האמן ביהוה = ἐπίστευσεν ... τῷ θεῷ LXX). Cf. Hatch, *The Pauline Idea of Faith*, pp. 2 ff.

[8] Cf. *Dial.* 119,6. According to 92,3 Abraham was declared by God to be righteous on account of his faith, and in 23,4 it is said that he was justified and blessed (ἐδικαιώθη καὶ εὐλογήθη) because of it. Justin, however, does not draw the conclusion that believers in Christ are justified by their faith in him. According to 92,2 those who lived from the time of Abraham to that of Moses were justified through circumcision, and those who lived from the time of Moses on through circumcision and the other commandments; but the justification of those who believe in Christ is not discussed.

[9] Cf. ibid. 11,5; 23,4; 44,2; 92,3; 119,5.

Such belief has at first sight comparatively little religious value, but from Justin's point of view it is highly significant. He holds that Christ is to be accepted, because he has been divinely predicted by the Hebrew prophets. Abraham, therefore, who believed Jahveh's promise made directly to him, is the great exemplar of Christian faith and the forefather of Christians, who believe God's words spoken by the ancient prophets and by the Apostles of Christ [10]. Hence Christians are called « children of Abraham » and « the true, spiritual Israel » [11]. They will inherit the holy land with Abraham [12]; and no one will receive any good thing from God save those who are « likened in mind unto the faith of Abraham » [13].

Faith or belief in Christ marks the beginning of the Christian life. The Messiah was promised and pointed out by the prophets, and the various events of his life were foretold, in order that men might recognize him when he should come. In this way God provided for faith. « If one does not believe in him (i. e. Christ), he does not believe the declarations of the prophets, who proclaimed and preached him to all » [14]. Faith in Christ is thus based upon the utterances of the Old Testament prophets, which have been fulfilled by him. However, the miracles of Jesus recorded in the New Testament and the witness of John the Baptist, both of which figure prominently in the Fourth Gospel as bases for faith, are not used by Justin as arguments

---

[10] Cf. ibid. 119,6.
[11] Cf. ibid. 11,5; 119,5.
[12] Cf. ibid. 119,5.
[13] Cf. ibid. 44,2.
[14] Cf. ibid. 136,3.

for believing in Christ. The Jews' failure to understand the prophecies aright is the cause of their unbelief.

It might seem as if faith were entirely a voluntary act on the part of man; but in a fragment of a lost work Justin couples faith in Christ (*ad eum*) with love towards the Father, and he says that both are furnished by God [15]. In this respect he agrees with the Apostle Paul.

According to Justin Martyr Christ is the means through which Christians have come to believe in God. Thus he declares that the Jews not only slew Christ and repented not, but also that they hate and murder his followers « who through him have believed in the God and Father of all » [16]. The faith of which the apologist speaks is much more than a mere philosophical belief in the existence of God. It is rather religious faith, for those who have it bring their needs to their heavenly Father in prayer [17]. It is on account of their faith in him that Christians beseech God that they may exist again in incorruption [18]. Moreover, those « who through the name of Jesus have believed as one man in God the Maker of all » are « the true high-priestly race of God » [19].

---

[15] Cf. Iren. *Adv. Haer.* IV. 6,2. Irenæus quotes from Justin's Πρὸς Μαρκίωνα (cf. Eus. *H. E.* IV. 18,9). This fragment of Justin is extant only in the Latin version of Irenaeus, except the first sentence, which is found in Eusebius. Instead of the usual reading *ad eum*, which is adopted by Stieren and Harvey, Codex Vossianus, the two Mercer MSS., and the margin of Feuardent's edition have *ad Deum*. The context, however, as Stieren points out, clearly favours *ad eum*, i. e. *ad Christum*.

[16] Cf. *Dial.* 133,6. Cf. also 83,4 (δι' αὐτοῦ refers to Jesus); 116,3; 1 Pet. 1:21; Iren. *Adv. Haer.* III. 4,2; IV. 6,3. See also the addition to Acts 18:8 found in Codex Bezae.

[17] Cf. *Dial.* 30,2.

[18] Cf. *Apol.* I. 13,2.

[19] Cf. *Dial.* 116,3.

They have been divested of their sins, as of filthy garments, and fired by the word of his calling.

The Christian life abounds in distinctions and privileges of various sorts. For God has had mercy, « through the mystery of the Crucified », on every race of believing men [20]. Those who have faith in Christ are cleansed from their sins by his blood [21]. Believers are blessed in and through Christ [22]; he gives them gifts, « from the grace of the power of his Spirit », according as each man is worthy [23]; and they have the Word of God, i. e. the Scriptures [24]. Indeed, « the seed from God », which is the Logos, dwells in those who believe in Christ [25]. When a person believes, he receives baptism, « the bath of repentance and the knowledge of God » [26], and he enters at once upon the new life.

By virtue of their faith Christians are another race, whose beginning is Christ. They have been begotten again by him through water and faith and wood, i. e. the cross. Water, faith, and wood as means of salvation were indeed prefigured by the deliverance of Noah and his family in the ark [27]. In another passage it is said that « there are two

---

[20] Cf. ibid. 106,1.

[21] Cf. *Apol.* 1. 32,7; *Dial.* 13,1; 54,1. Justin regards Gen. 49:11 as a prophecy of this cleansing by the blood of Christ.

[22] Cf. *Dial.* 33,2; 121,1.

[23] Cf. ibid. 87,5.

[24] Cf. ibid. 63,5. It is better to take τοῖς εἰς αὐτὸν πιστεύουσιν as a dative of the possessor with ἐστι understood than to supply εἴρηται (Maranus), or λέγει or εἴρηκε (Otto).

[25] Cf. *Apol.* I. 32,8. Grabe conjectured πνεῦμα here for σπέρμα. Justin uses the Pauline οἰκεῖν rather than the Johannine μένειν to denote the indwelling of the divine seed. Cf. also 1 John 3:9.

[26] Cf. *Dial.* 14,1.

[27] Cf. ibid. 138,1 and 3. Cf. also 1 Pet. 3:20 f.

seeds of Judah and two races, as there are two houses of Jacob: the one begotten of blood and flesh, and the other of faith and the Spirit [28]. It was prophesied that in this new race of believers in Christ Gentiles should be more numerous than Jews and Samaritans [29]. When they heard the Christian message, they were « filled with joy and faith and forsook their idols and dedicated themselves through Christ to the ungebotten God » [30]. The idea that Christians are another race, differing alike from the Jews and from unbelieving Gentiles, or that they are the spiritual Israel, is of course by no means peculiar to Justin Martyr.

Christians are distinguished by their upright lives. They keep the divine precepts [31], they are righteous, God-fearing, and peaceful [32]. Justin thus describes the life of believers in Christ: « We who were filled with war and mutual slaughter and every wickedness, have each from all the earth changed our warlike weapons — our swords into ploughshares and our spears into implements of tillage — and we cultivate piety, righteousness, benevolence (φιλανθρωπίαν), faith, hope, which is from the Father himself through the Crucified; sitting each under his vine, i. e. consorting (χρώμενοι) each one only with his married wife » [33]. But in spite of their peaceful disposition and unwarlike mode of life no one can terrify or subject those who have believed in Jesus [34].

---

[28] Cf. ibid. 135,6.
[29] Cf. *Apol.* I. 53,5.
[30] Cf. ibid. I. 49,5.
[31] Cf. *Dial.* 40,4.
[32] Cf. ibid. 24,2; 52,4; 70,5; 131,5.
[33] Cf. ibid. 110,3.
[34] Cf. ibid. 110,4.

Finally, Christians are able to exorcise and put under subjection all demons and evil spirits [35].

It was for the sake of believers that Christ, in accordance with the divine will, was born into the world [36]. The purpose of his incarnation was in part to destroy the demons, but it was chiefly to effect salvation for those who should believe in him. His saving death upon the cross was prefigured by the healing wrought by the brazen serpent in the wilderness [37]. But in order to obtain salvation, which is conceived in an eschatological way, one must have faith in Christ [38]. Hence, according to Justin, righteous Jews who do not believe in him will not participate in salvation [39]. This harsh conclusion is necessitated by the logic of the apologist's doctrine of salvation. Furthermore, a Christian must not under any circumstances lose or relinquish his faith [40]; for to do so is to forfeit his chance of being saved. Although faith is the primary condition of salvation, it does

---

[35] Cf. ibid. 76,6.

[36] Cf. Apol. I. 63,14 (ὑπὲρ σωτηρίας τῶν πιστευόντων αὐτῷ); II. 6,5 (ὑπὲρ τῶν πιστευόντων ἀνθρώπων); *Dial.* 70,4 (διὰ τοὺς πιστεύοντας εἰς αὐτόν). In the last-mentioned passage the verb σωματοποιεῖσθαι is used, which recalls *pagrūthā* in Syriac writers.

[37] Cf. *Apol.* I. 60,3; *Dial.* 91,4; 94,2.

[38] Cf. *Dial.* 35,8; 47,1 f.; 94,2; 111,2; 138,3. Cf. also 46,1, where Trypho asks if those who keep the Mosaic ordinances and believe in Jesus can be saved. Justin then proceeds to show that the various prescriptions of the law contribute nothing to righteousness or piety. Faith in Christ, with the implications involved in it, is sufficient unto salvation. In 24,1 the writer speaks of Christians as having believed in saving blood (αἵματι σωτηρίῳ) in contradistinction to the blood of circumcision. Christ's death upon the cross makes salvation possible for those who have faith in him.

[39] Cf. ibid. 47,4.

[40] Cf. ibid. 111,2.

not by itself suffice. It must be accompanied by repentance and righteousness of life. Otherwise the moral fibre of Christianity would have been ruined.

Death has lost its terror for believers. « As the blood of the passover saved those who were in Egypt, so also will the blood of Christ rescue from death those who have believed »[41]. At the *parousia* death will « wholly cease from those who believe in him and live acceptably, being no more »[42]. Moreover, if any believer suffers a bodily defect in this life, but keeps faithfully the teachings of Jesus, he will then be raised up sound[43].

Those who have faith in Christ and have repented of their sins will receive the inheritance along with the patriarchs and prophets and righteous men of Israel rather than the unbelieving Jews who persecuted the Lord[44]. Believers will be with Christ in the Holy Land and will inherit everlasting and incorruptible blessings[45]. They will spend a thousand years in Jerusalem, « which will be built, adorned, and enlarged » in accordance with the declarations of the prophets[46].

The substantive πίστις is almost always subjective in Justin. Once, however, it is conjoined with teaching (μαθητεία) and seems to mean *fides quae creditur* — the substance or content of Christian teaching[47].

Christians are occasionally spoken of by Justin as « the

[41] Cf. ibid. 111,3.

[42] Cf. ibid. 45,4. Cf. also *Dial.* 100,6.

[43] Cf. ibid. 69,7.

[44] Cf. ibid. 26,1.

[45] Cf. ibid. 139,5.

[46] Cf. ibid. 80,5; 81,4; Cf. Rev. 20:4.

[47] Cf. ibid. 53,6. Cf. also 1 Tim. 4:6 (τῆς πίστεως καὶ τῆς καλῆς διδασκαλίας).

believers » (οἱ πιστοί) [48], just as those who do not believe in Christ are called « the unbelievers » (οἱ ἄπιστοι) [49].

In the writings of Justin Martyr, faith is primarily intellectual, i. e. it is belief rather than trust. Nevertheless, belief in Christ as the Messiah implies trust, self-surrender, and loyalty. It is the basic principle of the Christian religion as well as the most characteristic feature of the Christian life, and hence the various blessings which believers enjoy in the present or hope for in the future are ultimately due to faith. Justin, however, was no mystic, and he did not think of faith as bringing one into mystical union or fellowship with Christ or God.

III. *Tatian.*

Of the words which we are investigating, only πίστις, πιστεύειν, and ἀπιστία are found in the sole extant work of Tatian. The verb greatly predominates over the substantives, each of which occurs but once. Πιστεύειν, however, never has a specifically Christian connotation, and therefore only πίστις and ἀπιστία will be considered here.

Faith is the principle or power which actuates Christians. Tatian tells his pagan readers that « men, after the loss of immortality, have vanquished death by the death that is through faith » [50]. The writer is probably thinking of the martyrs, who by virtue of their faith overcame death by meeting it bravely and hopefully.

---

[48] Cf. *Dial.* 35,3; 47,2.

[49] Cf. ibid. 91,3.

[50] Cf. Tatian *Orat. ad Graecos* 15,4. Cf. also 1 John 5:4, where Christian faith is declared to be « the victory which has overcome the world ».

Tatian says nothing about the origin or beginning of faith and nothing further about its working, what it does, or what it enables one to achieve. Its object is not stated, and its character is not described. Nevertheless, faith is understood by him to be the basic principle of the Christian religion and the distinctive characteristic of the Christian life. It is doubtless based upon belief or conviction, but it is clearly more than either of them. The unbelief of the apologist's pagan readers is opposed to the Christians' faith and is incompatible with it [51].

IV. *Melito.*

The substantive πίστις occurs twice in a Greek fragment of Melito, and the verb *haimen* is found once in a Syriac fragment. None of the other words which we are studying are used in the scanty remains of this apologist's writings.

The substantive is employed objectively in both cases to denote the substance or content of Christian teaching. Melito writes thus in the preface to his *Extracts* : « Since thou hast frequently, out of zeal for the word, requested that extracts be made for thee from both the law and the prophets concerning the Saviour and all our faith, and furthermore also hast wished to acquire accurate information about the ancient books, how many they are in number and of what sort they are as regards order ; I have taken pains to perform such a task, knowing thy zeal concerning the faith and thy desire for knowledge concerning the word » [52].

---

[51] Cf. ibid. 32,2.

[52] Cf. Eus. *H. E.* IV. 26,13.

It is said in one of the Syriac fragments that Christ was not believed in by people, i. e. the Jews did not believe in him and accept him as the Messiah [53]. Belief in Christ as the Messiah is primarily intellectual, but it also includes trust and loyalty.

V. *Athenagoras.*

All the words which we are studying are found in the writings of Athenagoras, but they are not employed in a specifically religious or theological sense. None but the substantive πίστις needs to be discussed here.

The connotation of the word is always intellectual, even when it is used in connection with religious matters. In other words it signifies belief rather than trust. Twice it is subjective, and denotes belief or conviction concerning the resurrection of the dead [54]. The writer holds that the latter can be proved by certain infallible arguments. On the other hand πίστις once has the objective sense, meaning that which is believed; and it is applied to the Christians' belief that there is one God, who is from the beginning, and who is the Creator of the universe [55].

---

[53] Cf. Otto, *Corpus Apologetarum Christianorum,* IX., p. 499 (*Frag.* XV) *ethhaiman* represents ἐπιστεύθη. Cf. also 1 Tim. 3 : 16; Justin, *Apol.* I. 40,7; 54,3; 56,1; Irenaeus, *Frag. Arm.* II. (XXXI Harvey); *Ep. ad Diogn.* 11,3.

[54] Cf. *De Res.* 14,15. So, too, ἀπιστία is twice used of unbelief in regard to the resurrection (*De Res.* 1,2).

[55] Cf. *Leg.* 8,1.

VI. *Theophilus of Antioch.*

All the words which we are investigating except the adjective πιστός are found in the treatise of Theophilus addressed to Autolycus. The writer uses both the substantive πίστις and the verb πιστεύειν of faith or trust in God [56], but it happens that neither of them is employed in reference to Christ.

After setting forth the greatness and power of the Creator Theophilus says: « But before all let faith and the fear of God have the precedence in your heart, and then you will understand these things » [57]. In other words without trust and reverential fear one cannot understand or appreciate God or his works. In another passage faith is associated with righteousness and the doing of good, and these three are mentioned as the means by which a man may please God [58]. Finally, future blessedness is made conditional upon having faith in God in the present life. « For », says Theophilus, « God will raise your flesh immortal with your soul; and then, having become immortal, you will see the Immortal One, if now you believe in him» [59].

---

[56] Πίστις has no adjunct of any kind; and πιστεύειν, meaning 'to believe in', takes the dative.

[57] Cf. *Ad Autol.* 1,7. Cf. also 1,14.

[58] Cf. ibid. 2,38.

[59] Cf. ibid. 1,7. All the manuscripts (VBP) have ἀνεγείρει here; but ἀνεγερεῖ seems preferable, for the present instead of the future is harsh in collocation with the following ὄψῃ. Grabe, according to Wolf (*Theophili Libri iii ad Autolycum graece,*

The connotation of the negative words, ἀπιστία, ἀπιστεῖν, and ἄπιστος, is intellectual rather than religious, and they throw no light on Theophilus's idea of faith.

Faith, in the passages considered above, is essentially trust — the right attitude of mind and heart towards God. There is, however, no trace of mysticism in it. Trust and reverence are elements of primary importance in the religious consciousness; and when they are conjoined with righteousness and the doing of good, they constitute the basis for a healthy religious and moral life [60].

---

p. 33), conjectured ἀναγερεῖ (from ἀναγείρειν); but Otto, following the manuscripts, reads ἀνεγείρει.

[60] The idea of faith in Theophilus is discussed by Paul in *Jahrbücher für protestantische Theologie*, i., pp. 546 ff.

APPENDIX.

I. *The Kerygma of Peter.*

In the Kerygma of Peter the object of faith is sometimes God and sometimes Christ, and in both cases πίστις includes trust as well as mere belief. It was universally believed among Christians that the Hebrew prophets spoke under divine inspiration. When the Apostles recognized that the ancient predictions concerning Christ, his advent, passion, resurrection, and ascension, had actually been fulfilled, they believed in God[1]. Second century Christianity was based on the fulfillment of prophecy in Christ. The argument worked in both directions. Men believed in God because the prophecies, of which he was the author, were fulfilled in the life of Christ; and conversely they believed in Christ because he fulfilled the prophecies.

Forgiveness of sins is promised on two conditions, viz. repentance and faith in God through Christ[2]. Sin is transgression of God's law, and repentance is sorrow for sin coupled with an earnest resolve to avoid wrongdoing in the future. Faith on the other hand is primarily religious, being

[1] Cf. Clem. Alex., *Strom.* VI. 15,128 (Preuschen, *Antilegomena*[2], p. 91).

[2] Cf. ibid. *Strom.* VI. 5,43 (*Preuschen, op. cit.*, p. 90). Καί is rightly inserted after μετανοῆσαι by Stählin.

the right attitude of mind and heart towards God. In the *Kerygma* of Peter, as in Justin Martyr and Irenaeus [3], faith in God is mediated by faith in Christ. We have just seen that these two are interdependent.

Faith in Christ arises from hearing the Gospel preached. It enables those who possess it to reveal future events, and it leads to salvation [4]. That πίστις comes from hearing (ἀκοή), and that it issues in salvation (σωτηρία) are commonplaces of Christian teaching from the beginning. But the idea that believers should reveal future events through faith in Christ is unusual. It belongs in the same category with the wonderful signs which are to be wrought in Christ's name according to the promise contained in the ungenuine conclusion to the Gospel according to Mark [5].

II. *The Apocalypse of Peter.*

The adjective πιστός occurs once in the Akhmîm fragment of the Apocalypse of Peter. We cannot be sure whether the writer meant it to be understood in the active or the passive sense, though the latter seems more probable [6]. The faithful (or believers in Christ) are distinguished from the false prophets, « the sons of destruction » and « of lawlessness », who will teach manifold doctrines leading to destruction. The Lord declares that « God will then come to my faithful ones (or to those who believe in me), who hunger and thirst and are afflicted and prove their souls in this life, and he

---

[3] Cf. Justin, *Dial.* 116,3; 133,6; Iren., *Adv. Haer.* III. 4,2.

[4] Cf. Clem. Alex., *Strom.* VI. 6,48 (Preuschen, *op. cit.*, p. 90).

[5] Cf. [Mk.] 16 : 17 f.

[6] Active (Preuschen); passive (Rutherfurd, Weinel).

will condemn the sons of lawlessness »[7]. Such is the reward of faithfulness (or of faith). Faithfulness springs from faith, and faith produces faithfulness.

III. *The Epistle to Diognetus* (I—X)[8].

The substantive πίστις occurs twice in the genuine part of the Epistle to Diognetus. In the first instance it denotes a trustful and receptive attitude of mind, which is the indispensable condition of revelation. Unless man has faith, God cannot make himself known. « No man has either seen or known him, but he has revealed himself. And he has revealed himself through faith, to which alone it has been

[7] Cf. *Apoc. Petri* 3 (Preuschen, *op. cit.*, p. 84).

[8] The Epistle to Diognetus should probably be assigned to the end of the second century or to the third. Cf. Zahn in *Göttingische gelehrte Anzeigen*, 1873, pp. 115 f.; Seeberg in Zahn's *Forschungen zur Geschichte des neutestamentlichen Kanons*, V., p. 243; Harnack, *Die Chronologie der altchristlichen Litteratur*, I., pp. 514 f.; Jordan, *Geschichte der altchristlichen Literatur*, p. 157. Krüger, however, thinks the work was very probably written in the second century, perhaps before the uprising of the Jews under Bar-Cochba (cf. *Geschichte der altchristlichen Literatur*, 1-2, p. 85). The last two chapters of the epistle (XI-XII) are very different in style and though from those which precede them, and they are undoubtedly by another hand. The Strasbourg manuscript had the following note in the margin at this point: καὶ ὧδε ἐγκοπὴν εἶχε τὸ ἀντίγραφον. Practically all scholars agree in regarding chapters XI and XII as the work of another writer. Kihn, however, defends them as « an integral and necessary part of the letter » (cf. *Der Ursprung des Briefes an Diognet*. p. 55). Chapters XI and XII may have been taken from one of the many works of Hippolytus, who was a disciple of Irenaeus.

given to see God » [9]. In the second case πίστις is used objectively of the substance or content of Christian teaching [10]. It refers specifically to what the writer has just said about the Incarnation.

Justification is viewed as a divine transaction. The lawless and the ungodly have been justified in the Son of God, and his righteousness has justified many such [11]. Nothing is said about the conditions upon which justification is based; but probably the writer would have answered, had he been asked, that faith and good works are both required. Certainly only those who believe in Christ could be justified in him.

God, having demonstrated the inability of the human race to attain unto life, provided salvation for mankind in Christ. In this the divine character was revealed, and men ought to trust (πιστεύειν) in God's goodness. This is what he desired them to do [12]. The writer does not say that men are saved by faith, but of course only believers in Christ can participate in the salvation that was wrought by him.

---

[9] Cf. *Ep. ad Diogn.* 8,5 f.

[10] Cf. ibid. 10, 1. The manuscript read here ἐὰν ποθήσης καὶ λάβης (the letters σης being in the margin). This is the reading adopted by Funk, Lake, and Buonaiuti. Others, however, have regarded it as unsatisfactory, and various conjectures have been made: ἐπιποθήσαις, καὶ λάβοις (Lachmann); ἐὰν ποθῇς, κατάλαβε (Gebhardt); ἐὰν ποθήσῃς, καταλάβοις ἄν (Gildersleeve); ἐὰν ποθήσῃς, καὶ λήψῃ (Otto); ἐὰν ποθήσῃς, καὶ λαβέ (Kihn). It is better, with Krenkel and Lake, to retain the reading of the manuscript and assume that the apodosis has dropped out after πατρός.

[11] Cf. ibid. 9,4 and 5.

[12] Cf. ibid. 9,6.

IV. *The Epistola Apostolorum.*

Faith is frequently mentioned in the Coptic (Akhmîmic) version of the work known as the Epistola Apostolorum [13]. The substantive *pistis* and the verb *pisteye* occur respectively five times and twenty-six times, but the Coptic word *nahte* is not used either in the substantival or in the verbal sense [14]. The adjectives *pistos* and *apistos* are each found once; and the Coptic *anahte*, which corresponds to the Greek ἄπιστος, appears twice.

The object of faith, whether it be expressed or under-

---

[13] For the Coptic text, a German translation, and a thorough discussion of this document cf. C. Schmidt in *Texte und Untersuchungen*, Dritte Reihe, XIII. See also Lake in *The Harvard Theological Review*, XIV., pp. 15 ff. For the Ethiopic text, edited and translated into French by Guerrier, cf. Graffin and Nau, *Patrologia Orientalis*, IX., 3. The scanty remains of a Latin version can be seen in the above-mentioned work of Schmidt, pp. 21 f. The manuscript containing the Coptic translation of the Epistola, which is now at the Institut de la Mission Archéologique Française in Cairo, is written on papyrus and is ascribed to the end of the fourth or the beginning of the fifth century. It has unfortunately been considerably damaged. Lake (in *op. cit.*, p. 17) says: « The Coptic is an incomplete manuscript of a better text, while the Ethiopic is a complete manuscript of a worse text. Both are based, directly or indirectly, on a lost Greek original from which the Latin palimpsest, unfortunately only a small fragment, was also derived ».

[14] *Pistis* nowhere takes an adjunct. When *pisteye* means 'to believe' or 'put credence in', the verb may be used absolutely (7,9); or it may take an object introduced by the preposition *n*- (3,5; 26,4); or it may be followed by a *dje*-clause (3, 1; 17, 15; 25,8); or it may take an object introduced by *n*- and also be followed by a *dje*-clause (2,14 f.; 3,2).

stood, is in most cases Christ [15]; but sometimes, as in the Fourth Gospel, faith in Christ is conjoined with faith in God [16].

Faith is not thought of as a divine gift. On the contrary it is a voluntary act on the part of the individual, something that he can have if he will [17], and it is produced by the preaching of the gospel [18]. As in the Fourth Gospel and Justin Martyr, faith is belief rather than trust.

Faith is central and fundamental in the writer's conception of Christianity. He who believes in Christ through the preaching of the Apostles will receive from them through Christ « the light of the seal (*sphragis*) and baptism [19] ». Justification in the theological sense is not mentioned [20], but salvation results from faith. Believers obtain forgiveness of sins and salvation — blessings which Christ also conferred upon the righteous men and prophets in the lower world [21].

---

15 When *pisteye* means 'to believe' or 'have faith' in Christ or God, the preposition *a* -, *ara=* is used with the object. (e. g. 5,5; 23,8 f.; 32,6 f.).

16 Cf. *Ep. Apost.* 23,8 f.; 35,5 f. Cf. also John 14 : 1.

17 Cf. ibid. 28,13 — 29,1.

18 Cf. ibid. 25,11–26,7; 32,5 ff.

19 Cf. ibid. 32,5 ff.

20 In 40,5 f., according to Schmidt's restoration of the text, woe is pronounced upon those who show respect of persons and justify the impious man for gifts.

21 Cf. ibid. 22,1 ff. It is quite likely that baptism was mentioned along with forgiveness and salvation in this passage. A lacuna and the word *n̄ōnkh* ('of life') precede forgiveness. The Ethiopic version has "the baptism of life"; and Schmidt suggests that *n̄pmay* ('the water'), which is of suitable length, has been lost. "The water of life" is baptism conceived in a truly sacramental way. Cf. ὕδωρ ζῶν in John 4 : 10 f. Schmidt previously proposed *khn̄ oym̄tan* ('in rest').

These believed when he preached to them in Hades, for otherwise they could not have been forgiven or saved. Moreover, as God raised Christ from the dead, so will the latter also do to all those who believe [22]. He will bring them to heaven, to the place which the Father has prepared for the elect, and they will receive « the elect kingdom in rest and everlasting life [23] ». The judgment will follow the resurrection of the flesh and the soul, and there will then take place « an election of the believers who have done the commandments » of God [24]. Furthermore, the importance of faith is indicated in the interpretation of the Parable of the Ten Virgins. According to the writer the first of the prudent virgins is Faith, and the others are Love, Grace, Peace, and Hope [25].

Nevertheless, faith alone is not enough to insure salvation. It is necessary not only to believe in Christ, but also to do the commandments of the Father and the Son and to live uprightly [26]. He who merely confesses the Lord's name without keeping his commandments is not profited thereby. « He has run in a vain course [27] ». In other words, as the author of the Epistle of James maintains, faith must be accompanied by good works. The latter, however, are not thought of as springing from faith.

---

[22] Cf. ibid. 20,4 ff.

[23] Cf. ibid. 23,7 ff. Cf. also 5,3 ff.; 22,10 ff.; 25,1 ff.

[24] Cf. ibid. 20,10 ff. The spirit was probably not mentioned with the flesh and the soul in this passage. Schmidt at first proposed *mn̄ p̄na* ('with the spirit') in line 8; but later, following the Ethiopic version, he withdrew this in favour of *eyankh* ('living').

[25] Cf. ibid. 35,2 f. The foolish virgins are Knowledge, Understanding, Obedience, Longsuffering, and Mercy (36,10 ff.).

[26] Cf. ibid. 20,10 ff.; 24,2; 29,2 ff.; 36,12–37,8.

[27] Cf. ibid. 22,4 ff.

The substantive *pistis* is once used objectively to denote the substance or content of Christian teaching[28].

The adjectives *pistos* and *apistos*, like the Coptic *atnahte*, are employed only in the active sense. *Pistos* is used specifically of Christians as believers in Christ[29]. The negative words on the other hand mean simply 'unbelieving'[30].

[28] Cf. ibid. 27,2 f.

[29] Cf. ibid. 20,11.

[30] Cf. ibid. 4,1 f., 13 f.; 17,14.

Chapter VII.

I. *The Epistle of the Churches of Vienne and Lyons.*

The substantive πίστις occurs twice in the Epistle of the Churches of Vienne and Lyons, and both times it has a distinctly Christian connotation. The letter begins thus: « The bond-servants of Christ who sojourn in Vienne and Lyons in Gaul to the brethren throughout Asia and Phrygia, who have the same confidence (πίστιν) in and hope of redemption as ourselves, peace and grace and glory from God the Father and Christ Jesus our Lord »[1]. Πίστις can hardly mean faith directed towards or centering in redemption. It is rather the confidence or trust which believers have that they have been redeemed by the redemptive work of Christ and are destined to partake in the blessings secured by it. The content or character of redemption is not stated; because, being a common Christian concept, it is universally understood. But it is future and eschatological, and it means salvation in the last day[2]. For these Gallic Christians and their brethren in Asia Minor, as well as for Pau land Irenaeus, Chritianity is essentially a redemptive religion.

[1] Eus. *H. E.* V. 1,3. Πίστις is conjoined with ἐλπίς, and the objective genitive τῆς ἀπολυτρώσεως depends upon both substantives.

[2] Cf. Eph. 1 : 14; 4 : 30. See Holtzmann, *Neutestamentliche Theologie* [2], II., p. 285, note 2.

Later in the epistle πίστις is used without any adjunct to denote the believer's attitude towards Christ [3]. It is not *fides quae creditur* — the substance or content of Christian teaching [4]. Πίστις is subjective, and is at heart trust; and trust in Christ involves devotion and loyalty to him [5]. Hence those who have πίστις are able to endure persecution, but those who are without it fall away in time of trial.

Christ, the great example of the witnesses in Lyons and Vienne, is called, as in Revelation, « the faithful and true witness » [6]. However, the Scriptural phrase is not used in its original sense. To the author of the Apocalypse Christ was « the trustworthy and true witness » of a divine revelation, which was guaranteed by his character; whereas in the Epistle of the Churches of Vienne and Lyons he is the divine exemplar whom his followers should imitate, but to whom they shrink to be compared by allowing themselves to be called witnesses. Μάρτυς is a title which should be reserved for him alone. Nevertheless, those Christians who had borne

---

[3] Cf Eus. *H. E.* V. 1, 48.

[4] This idea is expressed by the perfect passive participle of πιστεύειν in Eus. *H. E.* V. 1,56. Valesius renders τῶν πεπιστευμένων by « *eorum quae credebat bonorum* »; and Crusè translates τὴν ἐλπίδα καὶ ἐποχὴν τῶν πεπιστευμένων somewhat freely by « her firm hope, confidence, faith ». Lord Hailes and Dr. Mc Giffert err in taking the verb in the sense of 'entrust'. Τὰ πεπιστευμένα are the things which have been believed, i. e. the various beliefs that make up the Christian faith.

[5] Cf. ibid. V. 1,41 (τοὺς πιστεύοντας εἰς αὐτόν, i. e. Χριστόν).

[6] Cf. ibid. V. 2,3. The words τῷ πιστῷ καὶ ἀληθινῷ μάρτυρι are a reminiscence of Rev. 3 : 14. Πιστεύειν also means 'to believe' or 'credit' (Eus. *H. E.* V. 1,14); and it is once used in the passive in the sense of being 'entrusted' with something (Eus. *H. E.* V. 1,29).

witness to the faith by their sufferings or death were commonly styled « witnesses » in a specific sense [7].

II. *Irenaeus.*

Faith plays a very prominent and important part in Irenaeus's conception of Christianity. It is indeed one of his fundamental ideas, and there can be no doubt that all the words which we are studying were used in the original form of the *Adversus Haereses* [8].

Πίστις means both 'belief' and 'trust'. In some passages the word has the former meaning, and in others the latter, according as its connotation is primarily intellectual or religious.

The object of faith, as one might expect in a Christian writer of the latter part of the second century, is sometimes God [9], sometimes Christ [10], and sometimes the Holy Spirit [11]. Irenæus thinks of faith in God as mediated either through

[7] On the use of the word μάρτυς in early Christian writers cf. Mc Giffert, *The Church History of Eusebius*, p. 164, note 15.

[8] Πίστις is generally used absolutely. It never takes an objective genitive, but it is found five times with a prepositional phrase introduced by εἰς (*Adv. Haer.* I. 3,6 [God and Christ]; 10,1 [God, Christ, and the Holy Spirit]; III. 12,2 [Christ]; IV. 33,7 [God]; *Frag.* XXV [Christ]. No other preposition is employed in this connection. Πιστεύειν is used once with the dative τῷ θεῷ (*Adv. Haer.* IV. 5,3 = Gen. 15:6) and once with εἰς τὸν υἱὸν τοῦ θεοῦ (ibid. III. 12,2). No attempt has been made to draw conclusions concerning grammatical usage from the Latin version or from the Syriac fragments.

[9] Cf. e. g. Iren. *Adv. Haer.* I. 3,6; 10,1; IV. 1,1.

[10] Cf. e. g. ibid. I. 3,6; 10,1; IV. 1,1.

[11] Cf. e. g. ibid. I. 10,1.

Christ [12] or through the Holy Spirit [13]. Belief in the three persons of the Trinity, according to Irenaeus, was received by the Church from the Apostles and their disciples ; and, though she is scattered abroad throughout the whole world, she carefully guards these fundamental articles of belief and teaches them with unanimity [14].

Faith in Christ begins with the hearing of the Gospel message [15]. It is the individual's response to the facts and arguments presented by the missionaries, and it is based upon the conviction that Jesus fulfilled certain prophecies contained in the Old Testament. Moses and the prophets testified in advance concerning him ; and if one believes them, one ought to believe in Christ [16]. The Jews had a great advantage over the Gentiles in possessing the Scriptures ; but on the other hand the faith of the latter is of a more noble quality (*generosior*), inasmuch as they believed without the aid of prophecy [17].

In Jesus' time many believed in him because of the mighty works which he performed [18]. In like manner Irenæus, speaking of his own day, declares that « some surely and truly drive out demons, so that frequently those very ones who have been cleansed from the evil spirits both believe and are in the Church » [19]. The curing of demoniacs by the followers

---

[12] Cf. ibid. III. 4,2 ; IV. 6,3.

[13] Cf. ibid. III. 12,14.

[14] Cf. ibid. I. 10,1 and 2.

[15] Cf. ibid. II. 22,2 ; III. 12,14 ; 13,1 ; 14,1.

[16] Cf. ibid. IV. 2,4 ; 10,1 ; *Apost. Preach.* 67. John the Baptist also announced Christ's coming beforehand and « persuaded many to believe in him ». Cf. *Adv. Haer.* III. 11,4.

[17] Cf. ibid. IV. 24,2.

[18] Cf. ibid. II. 22,3.

[19] Cf. ibid. II. 32,4.

of Christ in his name was looked upon as a manifestation of divine power, and faith in him was a natural consequence. Those who believed were of course baptized, though this fact happens not to be mentioned [20].

« The acceptable year of the Lord », spoken of in Isaiah 61 : 2 and Luke 4 : 19, is « the whole time of faith », i. e., the period extending from the advent to the consummation. During it men hear the Gospel preached and believe, and by so doing « they become acceptable to God » [21].

Faith in Christ, like faith in God [22], is a voluntary act on the part of the individual. Abraham, the great exemplar of faith, « voluntarily and without compulsion (*sine vinculis*) on account of the noble quality (*generositatem*) of his faith » followed the Word of God and « became a friend to God » [23]. Similarly no one is constrained to believe in Christ. However, since God knows all things in advance, he knows beforehand who will believe and who will not believe [24]; but Irenæus nowhere speaks of faith as a gift of God.

The Spirit of God himself announced by the Apostles that he dwells within those who believe in Christ [25]. The Spirit is received at baptism through faith [26]; and by virtue

[20] According to *Apost. Preach.* 3 baptism is not only « for the remission of sins », but it is also « the seal of eternal life » and « the rebirth in (*or* unto) God. » The baptized are no longer « the sons of mortal men, but of the eternal and perpetual God ».

[21] Cf. ibid. II. 22,2. Cf. also *Apost. Preach.* 1.

[22] Cf. ibid. IV. 39,2.

[23] Cf. ibid. IV. 13,4.

[24] Cf. ibid. IV. 29,2.

[25] Cf. ibid. III. 21,4. *Inhabitare* probably represents ἐνοικεῖν of the Greek original.

[26] Cf. ibid. IV. 21,1 ; V. 9,2 ; 10,1 ; *Apost. Preach.* 42. According to *Adv. Haer.* V. 32,2 « those who have believed in Christ receive Christ » apparently by virtue of their faith in him.

of possessing « the Spirit of God, who purifies man and raises him into the life of God », Christians become pure and 'spiritual', or 'pneumatic' (*spirituales* = πνευματικοί) [27]. As the wild olive shoot, when it is grafted into an olive tree, « changes the quality of its fruit, ...being a fruit-bearing olive; so also man, being grafted in through faith and receiving the Spirit of God, ...changes the quality of the fruit of his works. » He is now no longer « flesh and blood », but a « spiritual man » (*homo spiritalis*) [28]. If this all-important change is not effected by receiving the Spirit through faith, a man « cannot inherit the Kingdom of God » [29]. Moreover, the Spirit of God is preserved through faith and a pure manner of life [30]. Concerning the reception of the Spirit through faith and the 'pneumatic' character of believers Irenæus and the Apostle Paul are in agreement.

Faith in God and in Christ, however, does not belong solely to the beginning of the Christian life; nor is it of a merely temporary nature, so that after a time it may be lost or abandoned without the most serious consequences. In order that one may obtain the blessings of the Christian life, faith must be permanent [31]. Steadfast faith in God and righteous dealing with one's neighbour are required of all those who are to be accounted perfect [32]. Moreover, not only in the present age, but also in that which is to come, « faith, hope, and love will endure. For always does faith,

---

[27] Cf. ibid. V. 9,2.
[28] Cf. ibid. V. 10,2.
[29] Cf. ibid. V. 10,2.
[30] Cf. ibid. V. 9,3.
[31] Cf. ibid. IV. 16,1.
[32] Cf. ibid. V. 6,1.

which is directed towards our Master, abide firm »[33]. With the passage of time faith naturally becomes stronger and more mature.

Righteousness, according to Irenæus is the fruit of the Spirit [34], which is received at baptism through faith and dwells thenceforth in Christians. Indirectly everything connected with the moral and spiritual life of believers is dependent upon faith. Through it they progress in righteousness [35], and their edification is in the sphere of it [36]. Love of God and one's neighbour [37], hope [38], fear of God [39], and obedience to him [40] are all associated with faith.

Irenæus, like Paul, contrasts faith with the Mosaic law and its works [41]. The law, which the Jews regarded as the peculiar glory of Israel, was the most distinctive feature of Judaism; whereas faith in Christ was from the first the basic and characteristic distinction of Christians. The former represents Judaism and the latter Christianity. The law,

---

[33] Cf. ibid. II. 28,3. Cf. also IV. 12,2. The Pauline triad of faith, hope, and love is mentioned by Irenaeus only in these two places and in *Apost. Preach.* 41 (faith, love, and hope).

[34] Cf. *Adv. Haer.* V. 11,1 (= Gal. 5 : 22).

[35] Cf. ibid. V. 10,1. Cf. also *Apost. Preach.* 3; 87; 89.

[36] Cf. *Adv. Haer.* I. *praef.* 1 (= 1 Tim. 1 : 4). The correct reading in 1 Tim. 1 : 4 is οἰκονομίαν; but Irenaeus has οἰκοδομήν (the Latin version reads *aedificationem*) in agreement with D* d f g m vg pesh. Cf. above, p. 63, note 40.

[37] Cf. ibid. I. 25,5; II. 28,3; IV. 6,2 (*bis*); 9,2; 12,2 (*bis*); 28,3; V. 18,2; *Frag.* XXXIX; *Apost. Preach.* 3; 41 (*bis*); 87 (*bis*); 89; 95.

[38] Cf. *Adv. Haer.* II. 28,3; IV. 12,2; 27,2; *Apost. Preach.* 41.

[39] Cf. *Adv. Haer.* V. 32,2; *Apost. Preach.* 3.

[40] Cf. *Adv. Haer.* IV. 15,2; 39,1; 41,2 and 3.

[41] Cf. ibid. IV. 21,1; *Apost. Preach.* 87.

however, was fulfilled in Christ [42], so that those who believe in him are not subject to it.

Although knowing, believing, and understanding are sometimes combined [43], faith is quite distinct from knowledge. Nevertheless, the two go together; for God has always revealed and shown all things to believers through the Word [44]; and Christ gives to those who believe in him knowledge of the Father [45]. In one passage doing the commandments of God and understanding are made to depend upon faith [46]. Moreover, the Lord grants the Spirit « to those who rightly believe in him and love him and know that there is one Father, who is over all things and through all things and in us all » [47].

As in Paul and many other Christian writers, Abraham is the great exemplar of faith [48]. He believed or trusted in God [49], and from his faith certain important consequences ensued. Christian faith was prefigured in Abraham, and he is its patriarch and prophet [50]. Since believers in Christ have

[42] Cf. *Apost. Preach.* 89.

[43] Cf. *Adv. Haer.* III. 6,2; IV. 5,1. In both passages Is. 43 : 10 is quoted according to the LXX. Μοι after πιστεύσητε, found in codex A, has been inserted to make the Greek text conform to the Hebrew.

[44] Cf. ibid. IV. 11,1.

[45] Cf. ibid. IV. 6,3.

[46] Cf. *Apost. Preach.* 3.

[47] Cf. *Adv. Haer.* V. 18,2.

[48] Irenaeus once mentions Rahab the harlot, who « was preserved, with her whole house, by faith in the scarlet sign » (*Adv. Haer.* IV. 20, 12). But Rahab's faith is in no sense parallel to that of Abraham. Cf. also Jas. 2 : 25.

[49] Gen. 15 : 6 is quoted by Irenaeus six times (*Adv. Haer.* IV. 5,3; 8,1; 21,1; V. 32,2; *Apost. Preach.* 24; 35).

[50] Cf. *Adv. Haer.* IV. 21,1. Cf. also IV. 23,1, where it is said that the patriarchs and prophets « prefigured our faith and disseminated in the earth the advent of the Son of God ».

the same faith that Abraham had[51], they are all his spiritual children[52], whether they be Jews or Gentiles[53]; and whatever benefits or blessings he received through faith are assured in like manner also to them[54]. Thus in the matter of faith the end corresponds to the beginning[55], and the patriarch's faith and that of Christians is « one and the same » (*una et eadem*)[56].

It was inevitable that faith, being the most characteristic feature of the Christian life, should from the beginning be felt to be a social bond among Christians. Thus Irenæus, using a military figure, speaks of men from various and diverse nations coming together « into one cohort of faith »[57].

The results of faith in the lives of those who possess it are very great and far-reaching, and its power is manifested in divers ways. Men of various nations, hostile one to another, have believed in Christ, and by virtue of their common faith have ceased to be enemies and live in peace[58]. « So great is the transformation which faith in Christ the Son of God effects for those who believe in him »[59]. Christians are indeed « lights in the world »[60]; and « because of their faith they are extremely wise (*perquam sapientissimi*) and please God, walking in all righteousness and purity and wisdom »[61].

---

[51] Cf. ibid. IV. 5,4; 21,1.
[52] Cf. ibid. IV. 7,2; 21,1; 25,1; V. 32,2; *Apost. Preach.* 93.
[53] Cf. *Adv. Haer.* IV. 25,1.
[54] Cf. ibid. IV. 21,1; V. 32,2.
[55] Cf. ibid. IV. 25,1.
[56] Cf. ibid. IV. 21,1.
[57] Cf. ibid. IV. 21,3.
[58] Cf. ibid. V. 33,4; *Apost. Preach.* 61; 72.
[59] Cf. *Apost. Preach.* 61.
[60] Cf. *Adv. Haer.* IV. 5,3; 7,3; *Apost. Preach.* 35.
[61] Cf. *Adv. Haer.* III. 4,2.

Moreover, the Son of God, who alone is perfectly righteous, « makes righteous and perfects those who believe in him »[62].

Irenaeus declares that the bodily infirmities of believers were healed in his day, just as they were in the time of Christ and the Apostles. Jesus' power still operated in the Church. When his name was invoked upon a sufferer who had faith in him, it was able to effect a cure[63]; but, as in the cases narrated in the Gospels, faith or trust in Christ's power to heal was the indispensable condition of obtaining relief.

Trust in God is also of vital importance. Man was created by the goodness of God, and therefore he ought to trust the Creator and submit to the divine will. If he will do this, he will become « the perfect work of God »[64].

By unbelief on the other hand all the advantages of faith are forfeited and certain terrible consequences are incurred. Just as God grants « a fuller and greater illumination of mind » to those who believe in him and follow him, so he inflicts blindness upon unbelievers[65] and delivers them over to their unbelief, turning his face away from them and leaving them in the darkness which they have chosen[66]. Those who do not believe in him and do his will are « sons and angels of the devil »[67]. Moreover, it was unbelief that led the Jews to dishonour Christ[68]. Finally, for those who did not believe in him after his appearance on earth is in store irremissible punishment at the judgment[69].

---

[62] Cf. *Apost. Preach.* 72.
[63] Cf. *Adv. Haer.* II. 32,5.
[64] Cf. ibid. IV. 39,2.
[65] Cf. ibid. IV. 29,1.
[66] Cf. ibid. IV. 29,2. Cf. also II. 11,1.
[67] Cf. ibid. IV. 41,2.
[68] Cf. ibid. IV. 23,2.
[69] Cf. *Apost. Preach.* 56.

In the sphere of religion faith is fundamental and vital. Forgiveness of sins, justification, regeneration, divine sonship, mystical union with God, and salvation are all connected with faith, which is thus of primary importance for the religious life.

There can be no normal or healthy religious life so long as one is oppressed by a consciousness of sin, because sin hinders the soul's intercourse with God. Irenæus holds fast to the apostolic teaching that transgressions of the moral law are remitted or forgiven through faith in Christ. God has ordained him to be the judge of the quick and the dead, and, as the prophets have testified in advance, «everyone who believes in him receives remission of sins through his name » [70]. When a person is in such an attitude of mind and heart towards Christ, he is in the right relation towards God, and his past sins are no longer a barrier between himself and God.

Irenaeus speaks of justification several times, and in general he agrees with Paul. Abraham believed or trusted in God, and he was justified on account of his faith. Works played no part in the transaction. This Old Testament example indicates that God justifies men by faith [71]; and the faith or trust by which one is justified is directed towards God [72]. Jews and Gentiles stand on the same footing in the matter of justification [73], for the Hebrew patriarch was

---

[70] Cf. *Adv. Haer.* III. 12,7 (= Acts 10 : 43). The verb *credere* here denotes faith or trust in Christ rather than mere belief in him.

[71] Cf. ibid. IV. 9,1 ; 13,1 ; 21,1 (= Gal. 3 : 8) ; V. 32,2 (*bis* ; in one instance = Gal. 3 : 8).

[72] Cf. ibid. IV. 5,5 ; *Apost. Preach.* 35.

[73] Cf. *Adv. Haer.* IV. 25,1.

justified in uncircumcision[73]. Therefore God « justifies the circumcision out of (*ex*) faith and the uncircumcision through (*per*) faith »[74]. Works are not required in either case. Indeed, in the *Apostolic Preaching* it is expressly said that « we are justified not through the (Mosaic) law, but through faith »[75].

Regeneration is conceived as a new generation given by God as a sign of salvation. It comes from Christ, who was born of the Virgin; but the individual must appropriate it through faith[76]. Regeneration does not spring from a seed supernaturally implanted in the individual in baptism. On the contrary faith is the means whereby one is able to

---

[74] Cf. ibid. III. 10,2; IV. 22,2; V. 22,1. Rom. 3:30 is quoted in each of these passages. Paul uses the future δικαιώσει, no *variae lectiones* being recorded. The Greek text of Irenaeus is not extant in any of these places; but in III. 10,2 and V. 22,1 the Latin version has the present *iustificat*. In IV. 22,2, however, Stieren and Harvey read the perfect *iustificavit* with Feuardent's MS., Codex Arundelianus, the two Mercer MSS., and Codex Vossianus. The other manuscripts of Irenaeus have *iustificat* here. For the difference between ἐκ πίστεως and διὰ πίστεως in Paul cf. Hatch, *The Pauline Idea of Faith*, p. 58.

[75] Cf. *Apost. Preach.* 35.

[76] Cf. *Adv. Haer.* IV. 33,4: *Quemadmodum autem relinquet mortis generationem, si non in novam generationem mire et inopinate a Deo, in signum autem salutis, datam, quae est ex virgine per fidem, regenerationem?* The Greek original is lost, and the passage is difficult to interpret. According to Grabe some words have fallen out of the text; but this does not seem to the present writer a necessary supposition. Irenaeus apparently means that Christ, by becoming incarnate, made regeneration possible for men. Cf. IV. 33,11: *Quoniam Verbum caro erit, et Filius Dei filius hominis*; (*purus pure puram aperiens vulvam, eam quae regenerat homines in Deum, quam ipse puram fecit*). Massuet thinks the phrase *ex virgine* refers to the Church rather than to the mother of Jesus but this is certainly a forced interpretation.

escape from the generation which is subject to death, and to pass over into regeneration.

Christ, being himself the Son of God, « makes those who believe in his name sons of God (*filios Dei*) » [77]. Thus the Christian ideal of divine sonship is realized through faith.

Irenaeus was a mystic, and religious experience for him culminated in mystical union with God [78]. Faith or trust is the means by which this goal is attained, and through it the believer is united to God [79]. Religious people « make their way steadily into (*in*) the Father and the Son through faith » [80]. Thus, as in the Epistles of Paul and the Fourth Gospel, faith itself takes on a mystical character.

Salvation is eschatological in Irenaeus. On the last day God will judge mankind, which has suffered from the serpent's wound since the fall of Adam and Eve in the Garden of Eden [81]. But that men may escape condemnation and be saved, God has graciously provided redemption for them in Christ. In order, however, that the individual may appropriate the benefits of Christ's death and participate in the redemption procured by it, he must have faith. This is the means by which salvation is obtained [82]. Its object is usually

---

[77] Cf. ibid. III. 6,2. This passage is a reminiscence of John 1 : 12, where τέκνα θεοῦ is found. *Filios Dei* may represent τέκνα θεοῦ in the Greek original of the *Adversus Haereses* (the Vulgate has *filios Dei* in John 1 : 12); or Irenaeus may have used the Pauline υἱοὺς θεοῦ.

[78] Professor Rudolf Otto of Marburg holds that the fundamental characteristics of mysticism are immanence, superpersonalism, and theopantism. Cf. also Hatch, *op. cit.*, p. 10.

[79] Cf. *Adv. Haer.* V. 27,2; 28,1.

[80] Cf. ibid. V. 8,3.

[81] Cf. ibid. IV. 2,7; 24,1.

[82] Cf. ibid. II. 29,1; IV. 6,7; 17,4; *Frag. Syr.* XXVII; *Apost. Preach.* 1. In II. 29,1 all the manuscripts have *corruptelam*; but,

Christ [83], but it is sometimes directed towards God [84]. Faith in God and faith in Christ are closely connected in Irenaeus [85], and psychologically they are the same. Upon unbelievers on the other hand dire punishment will be visited [86]. But faith must be accompanied by righteousness [87], for God will judge men on the basis of their deeds, and the wicked will not inherit eternal life. Faith makes salvation possible, and righteous living insures a favourable judgment.

Πίστις, or *fides* in the Latin version, is often used objectively by Irenaeus to denote the substance or content of Christian teaching [88]. This usage is well established in the second century, and no comment on it is required.

---

as Harvey points out in his edition (I., p. 359, note 5), *incorruptelam* is required by the sense of the passage. The preposition *in* has probably dropped out through haplography. In the following passages love is mentioned along with faith as a means of salvation: *Adv. Haer.* IV. 28, 3 (love towards God); *Apost. Preach.* 87 (love towards God and neighbour). Cf. also *Adv. Haer.* I. 25,5, where the opinion of the Carpocratians is given.

[83] Cf. *Adv. Haer.* III. 10,3; IV. 2,7; 24,1 and 2; 28,3; 36,4; V. 27,1; *Apost. Preach.* 27; 51; 52; 53; 69; 87.

[84] Cf. *Adv. Haer.* IV. 5,5; 15,2; 28,3; 33,15. *Ei* in IV. 6,5 and *eum* in IV. 6,7 are ambiguous.

[85] Cf. e. g. ibid. I, 3, 6; IV. 6,7.

[86] Cf. ibid. I. 22,1; III. 7,1 and 2; IV. 6,5 and 7; 28,2 and 3; 33,11; 36,4; V. 27,1; *Apost. Preach.* 56.

[87] Cf. *Adv. Haer.* II. 29,1; IV. 6,5; 15,2; 17,4; V. 9,3; 27,1. On the text of II. 29,1 cf. *supra*, page 138, note 82. In V. 9,3 it is said that salvation is impossible without the Spirit of God, which is preserved through faith and a pure manner of life. The Spirit enables him who possesses it to walk in newness of life and obey God.

[88] Cf. ibid. I. 10,2 and 3; III. *praef.*; 3,2 and 3; V. *praef.*; 20,1; *Frag* XXXV; *Apost. Preach.* 3; 6.

In Irenaeus faith is sometimes belief and sometimes trust. Faith in Christ is based upon conviction, and it is the root from which all the spiritual blessings of Christians spring. It is indeed the basic principle of their religion. Moreover, righteousness is the fruit of the indwelling Spirit, which is received through faith; and hence moral excellence is ultimately due to faith. Finally, faith is the means by which one comes into mystical union with God; and, as in the Pauline Epistles and the Fourth Gospel, faith itself thus acquires a mystical character.

Chapter VIII.

CONCLUSION.

The substantive πίστις and the verb πιστεύειν, as we have already seen, denote both belief and trust. Sometimes it is one and sometimes it is the other, and in some cases both ideas are present.

In Hebrew and Jewish religion, as well as in the teaching of Jesus and Paul, faith is primarily trust; but in the Fourth Gospel belief is the primary element in faith. This shifting of emphasis, which no doubt took place unintentionally and imperceptibly in Christian thought, was fraught with momentous consequences; for on the one hand it made possible the type of orthodoxy which is represented by Justin Martyr and the other apologists of the second century, and on the other it opened the door to the various forms of Gnosticism.

Belief is always a matter of intellect. In these writers it is no mere assent to authority, but genuine conviction. Nevertheless, when religion is based upon belief of any sort, it inevitably tends to become intellectualistic or rationalistic, and this is of course an evil; for if religion is to be the controlling factor in a man's life, it must appeal to his will and emotions as well as to his intellect.

Trust on the other hand is an attitude of mind and heart. It is directed towards a person, and it establishes a relation between persons. It includes self-surrender, dependence, obedience, and loyalty; and these are the primary elements of the religious consciousness. When religion is based upon trust, it must of necessity exert a powerful influence on life.

We have already seen that faith sometimes takes on a mystical character, as in Paul, the Fourth Gospel, and Irenæus; for by it the believer is brought into mystical fellowship or union with God or Christ. This, however, is by no means necessary. Whether faith shall have this mystical colouring or not depends upon the type of the individual's religious experience, and this in turn is determined by the nature of the individual himself.

Man finds himself in a world of mystery and uncertainty. He thirsts for knowledge and understanding, and yet by the use of his own powers he is able to comprehend but little of ultimate reality. The evidence of his senses is conflicting, and different facts point to different conclusions.

Nevertheless, he must live in this baffling world, and consciously or unconsciously he must take some attitude towards it. He may rebel against it, like Prometheus; but rebellion is futile, and in the end it destroys him. He may resign himself to it, like Job in the epilogue of the Old Testament drama; but resignation weakens him and makes him unfit for any great task. Finally, he may trust in a Power in or behind the world, and he will find that such trust enables him to live happily and usefully.

It is often said that in regard to religious questions just three points of view are possible. One may bow to the authority of the Church; one may accept the Bible as an infallible guide; or one may base everything upon one's own reason. Each of these three positions has its advocates. Catholics hold the first and orthodox Protestants the second, whilst modern liberal Protestants adopt the third [1]. These three points of view, however, may be reduced to two. The Church and the Bible may be grouped together as two different forms of external authority and set over against the reason. Between the latter and any kind of external authority there can be no middle ground [2].

But is not still another position possible? May not one simply trust in God or Christ, and make trust the guiding principle of life? It justifies itself when submitted to the pragmatic test. In other words it works; and when other expedients fail, it is not unreasonable to adopt a principle that works in practice.

One may believe that neither the Church nor the Bible is an infallible authority in religious questions, and that the reason is too weak and uncertain to be followed with confidence in such high matters. But one need not on this account cease to be a Christian or refuse to become one. Christianity unquestionably improves life in many ways, and to abandon it means incalculable loss both for the individual and for society.

The Christian religion is a great adventure of faith. We have already seen that trust is one aspect of faith, and that faith is at once the basic principle of Christianity and the most characteristic feature of the Christian life. If faith is to endure and be strong, it must of course be based upon conviction; but conviction may rest upon moral as well as rational grounds [3]. Experience teaches that faith works and

---

[1] Cf. Martineau, *The Seat of Authority in Religion.*

[2] Cf. A. Sabatier, *Les religions d'autorité et la religion de l'esprit.*

[3] On the nature of religious certitude cf. F. Ménégoz, *La certitude de la foi.*

enables one to live at one's best, and it may well be that by living at one's best one may gradually come to understand the meaning of things better than in any other way. Faith may thus prove to be not only a sound principle of life, but also a means of knowing God.

Vu à Strasbourg, le 27 janvier 1925.

Le Président de la Soutenance

G. BALDENSPERGER.

Vu :

Le Doyen

Eug. EHRHARDT.

Vu et permis d'imprimer :

Strasbourg, le 31 janvier 1925.

Le Recteur, Président du Conseil de l'Université

S. CHARLÉTY.

I. INDEX OF AUTHORS

II. INDEX OF SUBJECTS